A Best Half of Life® Book

Dr. Ruth's
Sex After 50

Revving Up the Romance,
Passion & Excitement!

WITHDRAWN

by
Dr. Ruth K. Westheimer

with Pierre A. Lehu

Quill
Driver
Books

Printed in the United States of America

Published by Quill Driver Books/Word Dancer Press, Inc.
1254 Commerce Boulevard
Sanger, California 93657

559-876-2170 • 1-800-497-4904 • FAX 559-876-2180

QuillDriverBooks.com

Quill Driver Books titles may be purchased in quantity at special discounts for educational, fund-raising, business, or promotional use.
Please contact Special Markets, Quill Driver Books/Word Dancer Press, Inc. at the above address, toll-free at 1-800-497-4909 or by e-mail: Info@QuillDriverBooks.com

Quill Driver Books/Word Dancer Press, Inc. project cadre:
Mary Ann Gardner, Doris Hall, Stephen Blake Mettee

To order another copy of this book, please call
1-800-497-4909

THE INFORMATION IN THIS BOOK IS NOT INTENDED TO SUBSTITUTE FOR EXPERT MEDICAL ADVICE OR TREATMENT; IT IS DESIGNED TO HELP YOU MAKE INFORMED CHOICES. BECAUSE EACH INDIVIDUAL IS UNIQUE, A PHYSICIAN MUST DIAGNOSE CONDITIONS AND SUPERVISE TREATMENTS FOR EACH INDIVIDUAL HEALTH PROBLEM. IF AN INDIVIDUAL IS UNDER A DOCTOR'S CARE AND RECEIVES ADVICE CONTRARY TO INFORMATION PROVIDED IN THIS REFERENCE, THE DOCTOR'S ADVICE SHOULD BE FOLLOWED, AS IT IS BASED ON THE UNIQUE CHARACTERISTICS OF THAT INDIVIDUAL.

Second Printing 2005 • ISBN 1-884956-43-2
Cover photo of Dr. Ruth by Pierre Lehu

Library of Congress Cataloging-in-Publication Data

Westheimer, Ruth K. (Ruth Karola), 1928-

Dr. Ruth's sex after 50 : revving up the romance, passion & excitement! / by Dr. Ruth K. Westheimer.

     p. cm.
Includes index.

ISBN 1-884956-43-2 (trade pbk.)

1. Sex instruction for older people. 2. Older people--Sexual behavior. I. Title: Sex after 50. II. Title: Doctor Ruth's sex after 50. III. Title.

HQ55.W47 2005

613.9'6'0844--dc22

                                            2005002826

I loved you with an eternal love.
Jeremiah 31-2

To that first couple in their 50s whose sex life
I restored some 25 years ago.

Contents

1

2

3

4

5

6

7

8

9

10

11

12

1

Your Brain Is Your Most Important Sex Organ

When you were a young man or woman, you probably listened to the Who sing the line "Hope I die before I get old" and thought anyone over thirty was to be pitied. Now that thirty is a distant memory, my guess is you've revised your position. And you know what, this time you got it right!

Are there drawbacks to getting older? Of course there are. But let me say categorically, when it comes to the subject that is my area of expertise, S E X, there's a lot of good news. Many people discover they have some of the best sex of their lives after fifty, sixty, and even after seventy. "Oh, come on, Dr. Ruth," I hear you saying, "You're pulling our leg. You're just trying to make us feel better about growing old." Wait a minute, I didn't say *all* the changes were positive, just some of them. And, if you are sexually illiterate and don't understand how to make the best use of sex at this stage of your life, your sex life can definitely plummet. So, while the prospects are good, it's going to take a conscious effort on your part to make the most of your potential. But you know what? That extra effort is an important part of the reason sex can get better. Let me explain.

Couples go about having sex for years, even decades, and all that repetition can cause them to fall into a rut. If their sex life is like that old gray mare and it ain't what it used to be, one reason might be sheer boredom. But, if you're going to have a satisfying sex life as you grow older, you're going to have to adapt to the new you, and those adaptations will relieve the boredom, thereby automatically making sex better. Now any of you readers who have been listening to me for the past couple of decades and are following my advice may already have kicked boredom out of the bedroom. However, I know books about sex are often treated like books about dieting. Millions of people buy diet books, a percentage of those actually read them, and an even smaller percentage follow the book's advice long enough to lose weight. So, while I've sold lots of books over the years and talked myself blue in the face on radio, TV, and at lectures, I am certain most of you didn't follow all my advice. You were having sex, and it was okay, at least enough so that you might not have bothered trying to change your ways to improve matters.

But this time it's different. If you don't change, your sex life may reach that stairway to heaven before the rest of you does. Now it's time to get serious. Now it's time to pay attention to Dr. Ruth so your sex life remains alive and kicking. And as I said, those changes may actually improve certain aspects of sex.

Since I want to begin by encouraging you, in this chapter I'm not going to get into the physical changes but instead will stay with the psychological ingredient, because improvements you make in this area will compensate for some of the physical changes that I'll be getting to in subsequent chapters.

Your brain *is* your most important sex organ

Why do I put more stress on what is happening above your neck than below your waist? Because the libido, the part of your psyche that causes you to become aroused, resides in your brain. You can have a brand new sports car sitting in the driveway, but if you don't have the key to start the engine, you're not going anywhere. On the other hand, if you have the key to the older sedan sitting next to it, you can go as far as you like. You might not go as fast or hug the corners as well, but you'll definitely get where you're going.

Now it's very difficult for you to control your body completely. Obviously, if you try to stay in the best shape possible as you grow older, it will help. But, for example, no matter how hard a woman works out, eventually she'll go through menopause; there's no stopping it. Yet you do have a lot more control over your brain. You can do many things to insure that your libido works properly until you're in your nineties. And by looking at the changes that happen as you get older with the right perspective, you can make certain your sex life is taking you where you want to go.

In other words, your brain can keep you in control over the changes your body is undergoing. But you have to train your brain in order to make sure this happens. You have to recognize the potential pitfalls and know what to do to avoid them. That's what I'm going to show you how to do in this chapter.

(If you're single or haven't had children, what I'm going to discuss next doesn't particularly apply to you, so feel free to jump to page 11 skipping the next few pages if you like.)

The empty nest

The main reason for the existence of human sexuality is to make babies, but babies, young children and teenagers, especially teenagers, can wreak havoc with the process that created them in the first place, their parents' sex life. When it was just the two of you, you could have sex any time you were together, as often as you wanted, and in any room in the house. Once children were in the picture,

Reality Check: You May Be Older Than You Feel

When what you can do physically fails to match what you think you can do, it causes what is called cognitive dissonance. If you felt your age internally, then you could more easily accept physical changes caused by aging. But since it is likely you don't feel your age, when you run into a physical limitation caused by aging, it's hard to accept, especially at first. You may get angry or upset, though you may not always recognize the cause.

When it comes to sexual functioning, another psychological component usually kicks in, and that's your ego. When problems arise with sexual functioning, at any age, it's almost always a blow to the ego. When they occur in older adults and it becomes obvious that their age is affecting their sex life, their ego can make them even more anxious.

your sex life was nearly squeezed into oblivion. It sometimes amazes me that couples have more than one child. And couples who have ten children, well, their ability to continue their sex life amid all the hubbub that must go on in their home is nothing short of remarkable.

But there comes a time in every couple's life when the kids are gone. During the first couple of weeks this exodus can leave you feeling depressed. But eventually it begins to dawn on you that, while you've lost your children, you've gained something almost as precious, your privacy. And with this new found privacy comes the opportunity to rekindle your sex life.

Notice I used the word "opportunity." Opportunities can slip through your fingers if you're not careful. And sadly, that opportunity is not there for every couple. Let me illustrate.

Case History: Harriet and Gerry

Harriet and Gerry spent twenty-five years raising three great kids who all went off to become successful adults. They'd devoted their life to them, helping with their homework, taking them to this lesson and that sporting event, planning complex birthday parties and buying them everything under the sun for Christmas. To get the money for all these extracurricular activities, Gerry had worked his tail off, which meant he'd spent many evenings working late. When he'd get home, his conversations with Harriet centered on the kids' activities.

As their children got older and needed less of their help, instead of spending more time with each other, both Harriet and Gerry took off in different directions. Harriet retired from her job as a teacher and took up tutoring, which meant her days were free to read or play tennis with friends, but she was busy until eight or nine o'clock most weeknights. Gerry had become more and more active in the community, which helped bring in new clients to his accounting business, but the nights when both halves of the couple had dinner together were few and far between. Half a dozen years went by like that. When their last child left the house for college, they discovered they barely cared for each other, a natural result of having spent so little time together. Rather than be drawn toward each other, they did their best to stay out of the other person's way. And that included in bed.

Gerry's nearly nonexistent sex life and concerns he had about aging, including the fact his erections weren't as sturdy as they'd once been, ripened him for the attention his new young secretary was directing his way. When he finally filed divorce paper, Harriet wasn't so much saddened as relieved.

Any couples whose children move out are faced with an empty nest. You may have heard psychologists talk about empty nest syndrome. Fortunately this is not something every such couple encounters. Empty nest syndrome occurs when there are already serious problems with the relationship. There are many couples who stay together just because of the children, though they might not realize it at the time. Kids, including teens, take up a lot of time, energy, and attention. You're driving them to soccer games, helping them with homework, shopping for them, worrying about them when they go out at night, and on and on. With some couples, "the kids" becomes the entire focus of their relationship. They don't do anything together that doesn't revolve around their children. They don't go to museums together. Or to the movies. If they go out to dinner with friends, he talks to the other men, and she to the other women. And all their private conversations are about the kids.

There's no doubt that a couple is supposed to care about their children, but not to the exclusion of their own relationship. Couples who suffer from empty nest syndrome may appear to have an ideal relationship to those who only see them outside their home, because after all they're fulfilling all their familial duties. But the reality is quite different. If they're not talking about the kids, they're not talking about much else. They watch separate TV programs. He plays golf all weekend, or watches sports. She makes plans with her girlfriends to go to the theater or play cards. And their sex life is just about nonexistent. They may not even sleep in the same bed.

Now what happens to such a couple when you remove the kids? Picture a house of cards when you remove a few from the bottom and you get a good idea. Instead of welcome privacy, they're facing an unwanted vacuum. They don't know what to say to one another. Not only may their love have evaporated, but they may not even like each other any more. When the kids were at home and he would work late most nights, it wasn't so bad for her as she had the kids for company. But when the same thing happens when the kids are gone, she begins to resent the empty house. And if he resented that she seemed to be shopping all the time, at least some of the shopping, he rationalized, was for the kids. Imagine how he feels when this excuse is removed.

I may be using some stereotypes here that don't necessarily apply to many couples, because these days she's just as likely to be the one who's out every night working late and he's just as likely to be spending hours doing something that doesn't involve her, like surfing the web. But the end result is the same: Where they tolerated each other when the kids were home, they now begin to actively resent the other's presence. It may not take long before they break up, leaving their friends and neighbors wondering how this "perfect" couple could have split apart so quickly.

Let me repeat, going through the withdrawal of empty nest does not cause empty nest syndrome. If you have a good relationship, after a short time in that empty nest you should draw closer together. You may even begin to dislike it when the nest fills up again during school breaks and summers.

Is there anything you can do about empty nest syndrome? The sad answer, at least from my experience, is no. I've had plenty of couples come to see me in my office who are victims of this condition and I can rarely help them. Empty nest syndrome can be prevented if caught early enough, but, in my experience, it can rarely be reversed once it has set in. However, if you are having problems as a couple that you think may be evidence of empty nest syndrome, don't just throw in the towel; go to seek professional counseling. First of all, it might not be full-blown empty nest syndrome, so there may be ways of saving your relationship. And even if it turns out you're too late, a professional counselor can help you to make the decisions you will need to make.

Since you're reading this book, I'm going to assume you're past the stage where empty nest syndrome poses a grave danger, that your relationship is basically healthy, and that you're still together. The key question for you is: Have you taken full advantage of your empty nest? In life, some people stop and smell the flowers or admire the sunset while others scurry on, missing chance after chance for personal enjoyment. How can you tell where you are in this regard? The simple test is: How's your love life? Did you notice improvement when the kids left or didn't you? If you didn't, then so far, you've let an important opportunity slide by.

It's not too late

Luckily for you, there's still time to catch up to it. The privacy of your empty nest hasn't disappeared. All you have to do is make better use of it. Here's one simple example: Many couples stop acting affectionate toward each other when the kids are around. They might give each other a peck on the cheek, but rarely more, usually because the kids will make some snide comment. You probably should have told them if they didn't like it they should go into another room, but assuming you didn't do that, when they were in the room, you were stuck with an occasional peck. But ask yourself if now that there's no peanut gallery observing you, do you kiss more passionately? If the answer is no, at the next opportunity, regardless of the room you are in or the time of the day, grab your partner, confess your love, and plant a big one on his or her lips. At first this may feel a bit awkward. Your instincts at keeping away from too much physical contact outside the bedroom may affect how you feel about starting now. But since those instincts are now useless, make an effort to throw them off. Break your pattern of passing each other like two ships in the night and develop a new habit of kissing as often as possible. Not only will you enjoy such moments, but they'll stimulate you for other activities later on.

✎ Tip:

One reason some couples don't let their passions come into play in front of the kids is it would excite him to the point where he gets an erection. This, understandably, is something they would prefer the kids not observe. In addition, some men feel that once aroused, they have to have sex ASAP. But older men take a bit longer to get an erection and don't feel quite the same urgency to act on it when they do. And, since getting an erection is good exercise for the penis (more on that in a later chapter), anything that will cause an occasional erection should be looked at as positive. So, while kissing doesn't have to lead to an erection, if it does, give yourselves a pat on the back.

What else can you do to break yourselves from the pattern of holding back when the kids were around? (You singles who didn't skip ahead might benefit from these suggestions as well.)

- Verbalize your amorous thoughts. I'm not saying you should suddenly start spewing all sorts of vulgar language. But stop swallowing those thoughts having to do with love and sex that pop into your mind. And, when making love, remember that no little ears are around to listen, so let yourself go and make as many loud groans and moans as you'd like.

- Slow dance. If the radio is playing and the right song comes along, fall into each other's arms, if only for a few minutes.
- Dress sexier. While you don't have to become nudists, not that this would be a bad thing, show a bit more flesh. Just try to do it with clothes that are meant to be sexy rather than items that show bare flesh because they're ripped and torn—unless, of course, your partner finds the hobo look sexy.
- Leave the bathroom door open most of the time. The less inhibited you are, the better will be your sex life. Closing the bathroom door shuts your partner out, a statement you want to avoid making.
- Break some rules. Have sex at 6 P.M., then have dinner. Take your shower in the evening—together. Wear each other's clothes.

You get the idea. Do things to surprise each other and break the routines you established during the decades the kids were growing up. Those limitations made sense when there were kids around, but they're useless now. Often the only way to get past them is to make a conscious effort at breaking them.

I'm not saying you have to make every day seem like you are reliving your honeymoon. I don't want to set you up for expectations that are too high. But if your natural level of arousal is less at this stage of your life than it was when you were first dating, it's more important than ever not to let your level of arousal sink to the bottom of the well. If you can keep it bubbling along near the surface, it will be a lot easier for the two of you to become sufficiently aroused when the time for sex arrives than if you've let your sexual batteries die altogether and have to spend hours recharging them.

A new need for foreplay

I think at this point it's important for me to mention a key fact in male-female sexual interplay that is often overlooked by many couples: Women take longer to become aroused than men. That's why I tell men to send flowers ahead of time rather than bring them to the door. If a woman has received a bouquet of flowers in the afternoon, either at home or at the office, by the time he steps through the door, seeing, smelling, and thinking about those flowers for several hours will have begun to make her aroused. Flowers handed at the doorstep, which, while a nice gesture, doesn't have enough lead time to act as foreplay. This doesn't change with regard to women as they get older. They still need time to get aroused. But it does change with regard to men, who will find they need more time than the split second it took when they were eighteen. So, while it is important for every couple to understand that foreplay should begin long before the couple gets under the sheets, it is even more important for older couples as both partners require some foreplay.

Too much togetherness

Can there actually be too much togetherness? It depends on the couple, but the answer certainly can be yes. If you're both still working or occupied with hobbies and other activities, this is not a situation you're likely to encounter. But if you're both retired and hanging around the home front most of the day and night, you might need to take a break from each other now and then. This is particularly true if one partner acts dependent on the other. In any instance, there's nothing wrong with going your separate ways now and then.

There is a risk, of course, that this time apart can be overdone. If a man goes to the golf course every morning and then needs to nap all afternoon, his partner may begin to feel like the proverbial golf widow. Naturally, similar scenarios exisst, where the woman spends most of her time in singular pursuits to the detriment of their time together.

Examine the issue of how much time you're spending together, talk about it openly so you both know how the other feels, and then try to organize your days and nights so both of you feel satisfied with the amount of time you're together—and apart.

Developing common interests

What if you don't want to spend much time with your partner? Maybe you're not actually suffering from empty nest syndrome to the point where you dislike each other, yet you feel unsatisfied with the time you do spend together. In other words, when you were spending two or three hours a day together, you enjoyed it; but now that you are spending eight, ten, twelve hours in each other's company, you're feeling different.

Important: For those of you who are not in this situation but one day may be, please don't skip this part. The advice I'm going to give applies to every couple, no matter what stage in life they are in.

It is vital for maintaining a satisfying relationship that you develop common interests. This can vary from a hobby that you work on together for hours every day, like remodeling part of your home, to something as simple as reading the paper and discussing the day's events. But what is deadly to any relationship is to sit together in the same room for hours without anything to say to each other. And I don't count having one of you filling the silence by saying whatever pops into your head as conversation. This can actually be worse than saying nothing at all.

Here are some tips on how to fix such a situation:

- Read things in common: newspapers, magazines, books, web pages. Then talk about what you've read.
- Learn a skill together, like cooking, painting, making pottery, tennis, or gardening. Then, when you're not actually doing whatever activity you've chosen, you'll still have something to discuss. And your choice doesn't have to be limited to one thing. If he likes to cook and she likes to garden, spend some time learning about both. Teaching a partner is a great way to share time together, and this can be much more rewarding than doing something by yourself. Just remember, a good teacher is a patient teacher.
- Explore the world together, even from your living room. Designate a season as your French or Greek period. Study the history and culture of the appropriate country. Rent travel tapes or DVDs, study the language a bit, pore over maps of the region, check out whatever related web sites you can find. Go to a few restaurants that serve this country's food and whip up some meals of your own using native recipes. Visit a museum that exhibits this country's painters and sculptors or check out books from your library on this nation's art. Read some of the literature—in translation, I assume.

Perhaps you can end the period with a trip to the area, but even if this isn't possible, you will have had a good time exploring this part of the world. And as soon as you're done, head for the next one.

For those of you who are thinking, "Dr. Ruth, isn't this a bit corny?" let me spice up this mixture a bit. Share a bottle of the country's wine, ale, or spirits. Pretend you're natives of this land when making love by giving each other foreign-sounding names and maybe doing some things in bed you normally would shun. One of the great things about going on vacation is you're free from some of the restraints of being home. If you don't believe me, take a look at the way tourists dress. Often they're wearing far wilder clothing than they ever would at home. By pretending you're away, you may not lose all your inhibitions, but with a little effort you can lose some of them. And by pretending to be Jacques and Georgette instead of Jack and Jill, you may find it really is easier to let loose. Try it and see what happens.

New-found inhibitions

You might think that the more time a couple spends together, the less inhibited they would be around each other. For some couples that's true, but for many others, as the years pass, they become more and more inhibited. And these acquired inhibitions often play havoc with their sex life. In order to prevent this from happening, or to reverse it if it already has, you have to get to the root of these inhibitions.

Body image issues

One cause for such inhibitions is body image. As you get older your body changes, and those changes tend to be negative rather than positive. It's easy for one or both partners to begin to view his or her body as unattractive, and regardless of whether or not this is true, this person will feel that his or her partner shares this negative impression. For example, a woman who has put on ten pounds may think her husband no longer finds her attractive, when he may actually like it or, like many men I've encountered, is oblivious to it.

Of course the media doesn't help things, with ultra-thin models everywhere and over-fifty models almost nonexistent. Having a few more reasonably-built older role models would certainly help alleviate this situation. Yet, while there is not much you can do about the content of the media, you can make an effort to combat such negative feelings at home by complimenting one another.

On the same front, some women feel they have to compete with the unclothed bodies that are shown in men's magazines and erotic videos. When they don't match up, their self-esteem plunges. While understandable, such feelings are not entirely rational. First of all, these women are selected for their nearly unattainable physical attributes and don't resemble the average woman in any way. Many of the women have undergone some type of surgery to enhance their looks, especially the size of their breasts, making any comparisons even more unfair. And it's not just women who suffer from such unfair comparisons. The males who appear in erotic films are often chosen for the size of their equipment. The average man who judges himself against these body types is in for a great deal of disappointment.

It is a mistake to make such a comparison between your body and that of models and actors and actresses. The best way of accepting yourself is to take a good look around, say while at a shopping mall; notice how few people measure up to those standards.

✒ Tip:

The most important thing I can say with regard to the issue of body image is to believe your partner. Very often I hear people saying they don't find themselves attractive when their partners are saying just the opposite. While I understand you may not be as happy with the way you look now as when you were twenty, the bottom line is that you don't have to attract yourself; you have to be attractive to your partner. If your partner still finds you sexy, then you are sexy.

Are sagging breasts or a pot belly more attractive than pert breasts and six-pack abs? I wouldn't even try to convince you of something so silly. But luckily you're both aging at the same time so you needn't be more ashamed of your aging body than your partner should be of his or hers. Of course if one of you has let himself go while the other spends hours every week trying to keep fit, this may be a problem. But, as I'm fond of saying, it's never too late. If you've let your body go, begin to work at getting it back into shape. Just the fact you are trying will give your partner a lift.

One potential outgrowth of body image problems is the person who has the poor image ingrained often hides his body. This ends up frustrating the other person, who still desires to see her partner's body. Naturally this situation then affects their love life. At the point where you should be following my advice to become more intimate, to deal with how the aging process can affect your relationship, one partner hides his or her body, making the whole situation less intimate. You have two people who need to draw closer together and one of them is pulling away. Sex is about letting go, and if one of you is holding back, it makes sexual enjoyment harder to achieve.

It is highly unlikely, if you have a body image problem, that you will make a quick about-face and whip off all your clothes at the drop of a hat. This is a case where both partners have to work together.

❦ Tip:

Remember what I said about sexual performance really not having as much to do with the part of your body located between your waist and your knees as it does with the part located above your neck? Yes, the genitals are sex organs, but if your sex life isn't working properly it's much more likely you have a psychological problem of some sort rather than a physical one. (This may not be true of males, but I'll deal with this in a later chapter.)

The one with the body image concerns has to be willing to make a few small gestures, and the other partner has to be as supportive as possible without exercising undue pressure. Certainly this person should tell his (or her) partner as often as possible how sexy she looks and how excited he gets seeing her naked. He should also make a special point of kissing or caressing the parts of her body he knows cause her the most concern.

One room of the house that may be helpful in overcoming this type of hesitancy is the bathroom. First of all, the bathroom is a room designated for nudity and this can be psychologically helpful to some people in overcoming their fear of being seen naked. Just the fact it is a smaller room can also make them feel less naked since they're less out in the open. And, with so many towels around, even if they're not protected by one, they can take comfort in knowing instant coverage is possible. And finally, the bathroom can offer a hiding place that is also transparent, the bathtub. By sharing a bath, especially one that has a coating of soap bubbles on top, a couple can be intimate without being too overtly naked. And while washing each other can certainly be sexy, it also offers a useful purpose, getting clean. The bathroom can serve as a place where the process of overcoming body image problems can at least begin.

Dim the lights

I recommend candlelight as another helpful tool. Candlelight is less harsh than either daylight or electric lights. And the flickering shadows thrown off by candlelight add a sexy aura to any room. Do be a bit careful with candles so as not to cause a fire, though. If you put them around the bathtub, there's probably less risk than elsewhere.

You might want to install dimmers on the light switches in your bedroom so, at the twist of a dial, you can have soft, mood-enhancing light that will also be less revealing, easing any body image concerns. A bulb with a low wattage in one lamp in the bedroom may serve as well.

The importance of good communications

There are other types of inhibitions that can be felt by older adults, but most of these are caused by physical symptoms and I'll be covering them in other chapters. Dealing with inhibitions of any kind requires one important skill and that is communication. It's always important for a couple to be able to communicate, but as I've been saying, it's even more important when undergoing a series of changes. Without good communication it is easy for there to be miscommunication, which can cause serious harm to the relationship. Let me give you an example.

Case History: Ginger and Fred

Fred had never had any problems getting erections. In fact, when he was a young man he was constantly embarrassed at school when his penis would become erect seemingly without a rational cause. But when he was in his late fifties, he noticed that seeing his wife Ginger in the nude didn't have the effect it used to. Fred guessed the fault was with Ginger. She'd put on a little weight and her breasts sagged a bit more nowadays, and, of course, he'd seen her naked body so often that he thought it just didn't have the same effect on him. He hated the idea of cheating, but he also couldn't face the idea of not being able to enjoy sex. One of the women at a company he called on in his sales business was in her forties, attractive, and recently divorced, and he promised himself to get to know her better.

To illustrate what was happening with Fred, I'm going to jump the gun and talk about a male sexual phenomenon. (You'll forgive me if I repeat myself when I get to the chapter on male physical changes.) It has to do with psychogenic erections. A psychogenic erection is one that is caused by some mental stimulus, like a sexual fantasy or seeing an erotic image. In young men, the sight of a pretty girl walking by can be enough to give them an erection. As men age, they start to lose this ability. Eventually they lose it altogether. They can still have erections but they need physical stimulation in order to get them.

What happens when a husband reaches this stage and neither half of the couple is aware of what is happening? Since seeing his wife in the nude no longer gives him an erection, he may think he's no longer attracted to her. When she sees that her body is not having the effect it always had on him, she may think he's giving at the office. He may actually think he needs to have an affair in order to continue to have a sex life. She may compound the problem by withdrawing from him sexually because she thinks he no longer finds her attractive. He may be too embarrassed to talk about it. Their whole relationship can come apart just because they're not communicating.

And the wrong kind of communication can make matters worse. If she says, with an obvious chip on her shoulder, "What's the matter, don't you find me attractive any more?" the situation will worsen. Furthermore, if he blames her, that's not going to get them where they want to go either.

Here's a better scenario. Let's say they are in the bathroom together and he's just come out of the shower and she's about to go in, so they're both naked. Addressing his penis, she could say something like "What's the matter big boy, don't you find me attractive any more?" with a smile on her face. At that point he might admit he doesn't quite know what is happening either. Maybe she could touch his penis, which might cause an erection, and they could then joke about his needing more foreplay. By keeping the conversation light, but also being honest, they should be able to get past this issue or any other that presents itself.

One in a thousand

Obviously, to be forewarned is to be forearmed, and a couple who understands the ebbing away of the man's ability to have psychogenic erections should have much less of a problem dealing with it, though it is likely they will still have to put out some effort.

Yet, that's but one of a thousand possible topics that could lead to miscommunication if handled improperly. The problem with such issues are they often blindside you because you're not expecting them. If your overall communication isn't good, your relationship is going to be vulnerable when one of these issues sneaks up on you. This means the best way to handle such potential crises is to make sure you're communicating properly at all times. If one or both of you have a habit of jumping down your partner's throat at the least little thing, then there are going to be difficulties as you approach the hurdles brought on by the aging process.

It's important to realize that many times such reactions aren't directed at the other party, but at yourself. If you're frustrated by the various changes that are affecting you, such as painful arthritis that makes it difficult for you to kneel down when gardening, it's easy to bark at your partner when he or she says something you find mildly annoying. This is similar to what teenagers go through when their hormones are kicking in. Teens can be testy when they don't really mean to be and don't quite understand why they're acting as they are. Some women have this problem all through their lives just before they're about to get their period—the dreaded "PMS." So it's quite possible an older adult having to cope with a bodily change, or several, may act testy now and then, though it is not directly related to the situation at hand. Men with spouses who exhibit PMS have often learned to ignore outbursts at these times of the month, and likewise many older couples have to learn to cope with similar temperamental issues. But to do this, there needs to be open and honest communication between the two of you.

You are more vulnerable as you get older and you're going to have to let some of that vulnerability show. I'm not saying to let all the world know or to tell your partner about every little ache or pain. All I'm saying is there are some health issues that are going to impact your relationship and the only way to alleviate this is to discuss it with your partner and make the necessary adjustments, adjustments that can't be made if your partner doesn't know what is going on inside your head.

At this point I feel I must address another cliché, and that's the one that suggests men don't talk about their feelings as much as women. Young boys learn early in their lives that if they fall down and scrape their knee, they're not supposed to cry. Strong and silent men are valued in our society. These early-life lessons do tend to make men less likely to talk about their feelings than women, so it's not totally a cliché. But I believe you can teach an old dog new tricks. Just look at how many older men have been perfectly willing to admit to their doctors that they're having problems with getting erections in order to get a prescription for a pill that will cure them of this problem.

Certainly if a wife believes her husband will never open up to her, he won't. He may need some coaxing, that's true. When it comes to sex, there are many women who avoid the subject, so it's often a two-way street. What both halves of a couple need to do is to look at the bottom line. If they can find a way of talking about their sexual relationship, they can have a thriving sex life for as long as they are together. If they clam up, they'll find themselves in a sexless marriage. And more often than not, a sexless marriage also ends up being less than full emotionally, so it's not much of a marriage at all. There are millions of older people who lead full and rich sex lives. The prize is there for the taking. All it takes is the resolve to communicate with your partner.

How do you open up the lines of communication if there seems to be a lot of static between the two of you? The first rule is: Don't speak in anger or try to place blame. If your sex life seems to be petering out, having a fight or series of fights, no matter what they are about, isn't going to help. Have any discussions on sex away from the bedroom, someplace quiet, with plenty of privacy and at a time when you're not rushed. To me, the ideal situation would be during a walk down a quiet country lane. The locale isn't crucial, but your attitude is. Don't start out with any preconceived notions. The example I gave earlier of the woman thinking he was "giving at the office" because his penis wasn't becoming erect in situations when it used to should explain why I say this. This is unexplored territory and you have to start with an open mind.

Don't be afraid to use the written word, either to get you started or to get your own thoughts together. If you spend some time composing a note that lists the areas you want to discuss, you can hand it to your partner and give him or her a few minutes to read it and think about it. Then talk about it. The advantage of a written note could be that you can lay out all your concerns, allowing your partner to see where you are headed. If you admit to your own failings in this note, it might make your partner less defensive and you might get further along.

If it seems like the discussion is not going to be productive, don't be afraid to stop and start up again at another time. At this point you've probably been thinking about this for a while, but maybe your partner needs some time to compose his or her thoughts. It's better to stop and start again than have frustration set in, which could lead to having the discussion end in an angry tone.

Finally, if you've made several attempts to talk about relationship and sexual issues and you're not getting anywhere, don't be afraid to seek out professional advice. If you had problems with, say, your eyesight, would you hesitate to get your eyes checked by an eye doctor? I don't think you would. There's not much difference when it comes to issues of sex and relationships. Sometimes the two parties can't adjudicate the problem by themselves. They need a referee or coach who has the expertise to bring them together. So, whether it is with a professional marriage counselor, sex therapist, social worker, or religious leader, get help if you need it.

And, while I know that for therapy to work both parties need to be involved, if your partner refuses to go, don't let it stop you from going. In the first place, this sends your partner a message about how serious you are. That alone may be enough to get him or her to join you. Another reason you may be joined might be that your partner will want to tell his or her side of the story. This may not be the motivation you're wishing for, but if it works, that's all that matters. Some therapists will call your partner and this can be useful in getting him or her into the sessions. But even if nothing will entice your partner to join you, at least you will feel better for having gone.

The Physical Changes
Women Can Expect
(Men: Don't Skip this Chapter)

I'm sure that just about every woman knows that once she hits a certain age she's going to go through menopause. I can be certain some of you who are reading this book have already gone through this stage, others are actively going through it, and others have experienced what is called peri-menopause and will soon be experiencing menopause for themselves.

Women have been going through these changes since time immemorial, but at no time in history has there been more confusion over this period in a woman's life than exists today. For eons, any woman lucky enough to survive pregnancies, privations, and plagues to live long enough to hit menopause, went through the changes, suffered with the hot flashes, and so forth, and that was that. Then medical science found ways to circumvent some of those effects via what is called HRT, or hormone replacement therapy. HRT brought good news and bad news, and exactly where we stand today is anybody's guess; certainly not mine.

I am not a medical doctor. Now I could do a lot of research, write down what I find, and then have a medical doctor or two review the material to make sure I hadn't put down anything erroneous. I've done exactly that in other books where medical information was required, and I will do it on certain topics in this book, but not HRT. The problem is, depending on which doctors I would choose to look at the material, I would get different answers. The medical community is sure HRT has side effects, some good and some bad, but there is no overall agreement on whether it is better to take HRT or not. So I'm not going to stick my littlest toe into these roiling waters. If you want to know more about HRT, read some other book, consult with your doctor, look up material on the Web, probably find yourself totally confused, and then make your own decision. And I hope you choose the right one.

The only thing I will say is that before we had HRT, women went through these changes, endured the hot flashes, coped with vaginal dryness, and all in all managed to deal with menopause. So doing nothing is certainly a viable option. That's what I did. I can't say it's the safest option, as the jury is seemingly still deliberating, but if you want to know more, then go ahead and do your own research. Just don't expect me to provide you with the correct answer, because I'm not qualified nor do I want that responsibility.

However, since some of these changes do affect a woman's sex life, I am going to cover those particular aspects of menopause. Those women who have gone through menopause and are taking HRT may not experience some of these changes, most specifically vaginal dryness. It's not really a big deal, one way or the other, and the remedy, using an artificial lubricant, is perfectly safe. But since menopause does have implications for your sex life, I would urge everyone to read this section, even if it doesn't apply to you. (And of course by everyone I don't just mean women taking HRT, but all you male readers as well.) Again, my area of expertise is not with the medical aspects but rather the psychological ones that have to do with sexual functioning.

Dispelling a myth

First let me dispel a sexual myth: There is no evidence that going though menopause means that a woman loses her sex drive. Going through menopause will bring many changes to her life, in general, some of which may have a negative effect on her sex life, especially if she is not forewarned and adequately prepared to deal with them. But menopause is not a death sentence to a woman's sex life by any means.

One group that has this no-more-sex reaction to menopause is made up of those women who never particularly enjoyed sex before they hit menopause. Rather than listen to Dr. Ruth, they followed the advice of that legendary Victorian English mother whose words of advice to her about-to-be-married daughter regarding sex were: "Lie back and think of England." For these women, menopause becomes the perfect excuse to stop having sexual relations, which they never liked to begin with. These women never had good communication about sex with their partners, probably did not have orgasms, at least not with any regularity, and so they actually look forward to the day they can say, "Sorry dear, I've gone through the changes so the door is now permanently shut."

This is a sad state of affairs for two reasons. First, it is doubtful the sex life of such couples was ever good, which is unfortunate, and second, it is possible that she has never experienced an orgasm. Having adopted this attitude, she certainly isn't going to in the future. But, while menopause may be used by some women to put an end to their sex life, it actually has very little to do with the quality of a couple's sex life.

Sexual boredom

Another group of women who decide to give up on sex when

they reach menopause are those who, although they may be orgasmic, are totally bored with sex. If a couple has been making love the exact same way for decades, and if he is the main cause of this routine and unwilling to accept her requests for some changes then she may use menopause as an excuse to stop having sex.

One reason couples fall into a sexual rut is that they don't communicate well, at least when it comes to sex. And if he hasn't listened to her complaints for the past few decades, the chances of him offering to become a better lover at this point in their relationship are poor. So menopause could spell the end of the two of them ever having sex.

Actually they're both cutting their nose off to spite their face. Sex should be shared throughout a couple's life, even into their nineties, and this type of reaction is a terrible waste and quite damaging to their relationship. Some couples in this situation find a way to reestablish communication. If they can't do it alone, as I keep advising, they should contact a sex therapist or marriage counselor.

Case History: Sally

Sally had always enjoyed sex, but after she went through menopause, her desire for sex seemed to disappear. She'd vaguely heard things about menopause, one of them being that it put an end to a woman's sex life, and though she hadn't believed it, it seemed to be true for her.

Of course menopause wasn't the only change in Sally's life. With her children grown and out of the house, she'd resumed her career as a librarian. Her husband had agreed that it was a good idea, as they could put her salary away toward their retirement. He'd also said he would help a little bit more around the house, but that hadn't turned out to be true. Sally yelled at him once in a while, and he'd do a little something, but it wouldn't last. Since Sally was tired of yelling, she'd pretty much stopped expecting help, but she resented having to work all day and take care of the house at night.

Physiological aspects

Are there women who had a good sex life and suddenly lose interest after they reach menopause? Yes, this definitely happens. And there is some evidence that the change in hormones affects a certain percentage of women in this way. If you are suffering from diminished sexual interest after menopause, this lowering of your libido could have a physical aspect, but the cause is likely to be psychological as well as physiological. In other words, there are some negative effects that arise from the decrease in hormone production, but this, by itself, shouldn't cut off all desire for sex.

As I said, I'm not a medical doctor, and even if I were, no one is absolutely certain how much the hormonal changes women go through affect their sex life. However, since the market for a hormone replacement drug is potentially huge, with approximately 30 million women having gone through menopause, the drug companies are busy trying to find out whether getting women to take hormones might have some positive effect.

Although testosterone is considered to be a male hormone, women's bodies do make it in small amounts, but the level decreases after menopause, which has led some researchers to look into whether testosterone therapy would help women who've lost their sex drive. The first tests were done on women who'd lost their ability to produce hormones following a hysterectomy and removal of the ovaries, which is where, in women, testosterone is made. Studies of these women who were given testosterone showed their desire for sex did improve. Another study of a testosterone patch for women (patches made for men include much too high a dose) also showed positive results. So far the United States Food and Drug Administration has not given its approval for prescribing testosterone for women to improve their sex drive, but it may happen one day.

Please keep in mind, if a woman loses some of her desire for sex after menopause, the reason—or reasons—is much more likely to stem from the combination of psychological forces that often accompany this period in a women's biological life than from a lack of hormones. And, while women who suffer a greater loss of these hormones are likely to benefit from such treatments, until the treatments are proven to be safe, I suggest that any woman who has experienced a diminished sex drive after menopause should not regret that a pill or a patch isn't available, because hormone therapies are known to have side effects, sometimes dangerous ones.

In the case of taking testosterone or other "male" hormones called androgens, the known side effects are usually minor, such as an increase in facial hair. But look how long it took for some of the negative effects of HRT to be discovered.

My advice is to deal with all the psychological issues first to see if you can't get your sex life back into full swing by making some mental adjustments, and only start looking at hormone replacement therapy as a last resort.

Let's consider some of the psychological issues I'm speaking about. One is represented by Sally's case. She went through menopause, but there was also another change in her life that was tearing at her relationship with her husband. Because of these negative feelings towards her husband, she didn't want to have sex with him. It's perfectly logical, but she didn't recognize what was going on because she was blaming her lack of desire on menopause.

The first thing a woman who has lost her sex drive should do, whether or not she is in her postmenopausal years, is to examine her life in general and see if there are any other changes that might be affecting her sexuality.

Ageism

Another reason for diminished sex drive is related to prejudice, and it's called ageism. There are common perceptions about older people held by the general public, even among senior citizens themselves, that are just not true. One of these is that older people aren't sexy. This is rubbish. Humans can continue to have and enjoy sex into their nineties. So, if they have partners who desire to have sex with them, of course they're sexy. This prejudice against older people is no less troubling than racism or sexism, and the stereotypes resulting from ageism can definitely have a deleterious effect on people, including you if you're not careful.

If you expect not to be sexy because of a lifetime of being fed the message that older people aren't sexy, this will become a self-fulfilling prophecy. There are some older adults who, when they feel themselves becoming aroused, try to stifle those feelings because they think it's not appropriate. This can be especially true if the person doesn't have a spouse. But of course it is very much appropriate. Your sex life is not supposed to come to an end just because you've hit a certain age.

Sex isn't just for procreation

Another myth that deters some older people is that sex is only for procreation and, therefore, once a woman has gone through menopause and can no longer become pregnant, she should no longer be engaging in sex. This, too, is nonsense. First of all, it would be totally unfair to women, since men can continue to procreate into their eighties and nineties and so only they would be "permitted" to have sex. But since such a small percentage of acts of intercourse in a person's life actually do cause a pregnancy, the idea that people are only doing it to have children is ridiculous.

Sex isn't a contact sport

One idea promulgated by ageism says older people are too frail to engage in sex. Again, this is utter nonsense. Certainly older adults must adapt to the changes that have occurred to their bodies over the years, but unless they have some severe health problem, the general changes that occur as we age do not make anyone too frail to enjoy sex. After all, while there is physical contact between two people when engaging in sex, it's not a contact sport where they're likely to do damage to each other.

Sex is actually good for your health. If you avoid having a sex life simply because you've come to believe that at a certain age sex is no longer appropriate, you won't enjoy the healthy benefits of engaging in sex.

Physical problems don't preclude sex

A mild physical problem can be magnified many times by the psychological aspects it triggers, so even if the underlying cause of a sexual problem ends up being physical in nature, you may find that the best way of overcoming it is simply by learning how to handle the psychological effects caused by this physical problem.

Case History: Carla

Carla had always been a very sensuous person, but she'd always wanted sex to be as spontaneous as possible. Since she could easily become aroused, this had never been a problem. If her husband wanted to have sex with her, she was quickly ready. After going through menopause, she still desired sex, but the fact that her vagina no longer became moist turned into a major difficulty for her. Though she knew better, she began to think that because her vagina was producing little if any lubrication she must not be aroused, and therefore she no longer was interested in having sex. And whenever her husband suggested that they use an artificial lubricant, she rebuked him, saying that it would kill all the spontaneity of their lovemaking.

Carla's situation illustrates what can go wrong with a woman's sex life after menopause. The vaginal dryness she was experiencing is a perfectly normal part of menopause. When a woman's level of estrogen decreases, she will experience a wide array of physical changes including a decrease in size of the labia minor, clitoris, uterus and ovaries; a thinning and smoothing of the walls of the vagina, which loses the soft folds and cushioning effect; a loss of vaginal elasticity, which may cause the opening to narrow and the overall length of the vagina to become shorter and narrower.

There will be an accompanying decrease in the amount of vaginal lubrication. It may take longer for vaginal lubrication to begin, and the amount will be diminished. All of these reactions stem from a lower level of blood flow to the pelvic region upon arousal.

In addition, vaginal secretions become less acidic, which can create an environment that is more likely to lead to urinary tract infections. This is called atrophic vaginitis. And the overall tone of the pelvic muscles may weaken which can lead to urinary incontinence, cystitis, and vaginitis.

As a result of these changes, intercourse can become a lot less comfortable and in some cases, can be painful. Adding to the potential for discomfort for the woman is that older men, including those who would ejaculate like jack rabbits when they were younger, usually take longer to have their orgasm. Such prolonged intercourse can actually cause vaginal bleeding. So, just at the point in her life when a woman might want the time for intercourse to be shortened, it lengthens.

All of these physical changes can, obviously, put a damper on sex. Some women react by avoiding intercourse as much as possible. But that is a big mistake, because while engaging in sex will not be the same as it was, it can still be very satisfying.

Remedies

One remedy for many of these symptoms is hormone replacement therapy, but as I stated, while there are benefits to this type of therapy, there are also risks. Another alternative for issues of vaginal dryness is to apply a hormonal pill, such as Vagifem, directly into the vagina. The hormones contained in the pill are a very low dosage. This type of drug is not a lubricant but instead restores the vagina's natural lubrication. Because of the lower dosage of hormones, risks are also much lower. This is an alternative that you will have to discuss with your gynecologist as this type of product requires a prescription.

A risk-free remedy for painful intercourse is the use of an artificial lubricant such as KY Jelly or Astroglide. Applying one of these lubricants will allow the man's penis to slide in and out just as easily and pleasurably for both partners as ever. So why is this a problem at all?

Other medications that may bring relief without the same risks as HRT are being investigated. There have been rumors that the drugs developed to help men, such as Viagra, work with women, but that doesn't seem to be the case. But just because those drugs don't work for women doesn't mean that other drugs that do won't be found. With the phenomenal success of Viagra, the pharmaceutical companies are hot to develop one for women.

Also, there is a device on the market called EROS CTD. This supposedly helps restore sexual functioning by drawing blood to the clitoris through vacuum suction. I have no idea if this device works, but since it is only available by prescription, if you're interested in learning more, ask your gynecologist.

Cause or effect?

Some women use vaginal dryness and its accompanying discomfort as an excuse not to have sex, but many of these women belong to that group we talked about before, those who never enjoyed sex to begin with. This is sad for them, but it makes their position against engaging in sex after menopause more understandable.

And then there are the women like Carla who, rather than deciding to adapt to the changes brought about by menopause, look at these changes as events to be challenged and denied. Instead of owning up to the maturation her body is undergoing and taking the necessary steps to alleviate its impact, she does nothing.

Yet another group of women don't know how to communicate with their partners about the changes they are undergoing. Many feel they are somehow to blame and rather than discussing vaginal dryness and explaining the need for an artificial lubricant, they simply try to evade sexual contact altogether.

And, since far too many men don't know vaginal dryness is a natural part of menopause and that their partner is likely to be experiencing it, instead of helping their lovers through this stage, they end up contributing to the problem by becoming angry at the sorry state of their sex lives.

Turn a negative into a positive

So what's an alternative? She explains to him what is happening and how they need to use a lubricant. He's going to agree for several reasons. First of all, it isn't likely he's ready to give up on having sex, so if there's a workable solution, he should have no problem going along with it. And , as I've already discussed, older men need physical stimulation to obtain an erection. Having his wife rub a lubricant onto his penis is definitely physically stimulating. And since they're both somewhat vulnerable psychologically because of their respective problems, working together in this manner adds to their overall sense of intimacy. In other words, this preparation for sex becomes part of foreplay and helps to increase their overall level of arousal. Couples who weren't engaging in enough foreplay before these changes arose may find themselves enjoying sex more than they ever did before. That's some silver lining.

As we've seen, the misconceptions and inappropriate attitudes developed over the years about the aging process may cause more damage to a couple's sex life than anything physical. So, while you

✒ Tip:

Studies have shown that post-menopausal women can prevent the loss of vaginal lubrication and diminish the thinning of the vaginal walls and the shrinkage of the vagina by engaging in sex at least twice a week. That's right, the more older women engage in sex, the less severe will be the symptoms of menopause related to good sexual functioning. Need I say more?

need to take certain steps to compensate for your changing body, more important are the attitude adjustments you must undergo to compensate for these physical changes. Adopt a positive attitude and your sex life can improve. Take a negative tack, and your sex life may disappear.

Worry-free sex

No matter what form of birth control a couple uses, and some even use several at a time, the worry about causing an unintended pregnancy remains, especially for the woman. But the arrival of menopause signals the end of that possibility. Many people, particularly women, find this very liberating. By removing the potential of unwanted pregnancy, sex can become much more satisfying. The only excuse for having sex is to share in the pleasure. The woman who once refused to make love anywhere but in bed under the covers before menopause may suddenly discover a new more adventuresome side to herself.

Sex 365 days a year

There's also the advantage of no longer having "that time of the month." While there's nothing wrong or dangerous in making love while a woman is having her period, it is messy and many couples avoid it. After menopause, there's nothing to avoid so a couple can have sex any time, 365 days a year. And if both partners are retired, they can have sex any time of day too, 24/7!

Combine these positives with the added privacy of the empty nest and you can see why many couples find that sex is better than ever at this time in their lives.

The other shoe

Of course there is another shoe to drop. There are some changes, either caused by menopause or just aging in general, that can have a negative effect on your sex life. In most instances such negative effects can be effectively dealt with, if not eliminated.

Two factors related to menopause are the hot flashes and night sweats that some women experience. These, in turn, may cause women to lose considerable amounts of sleep. If you are walking around trying to keep your eyes from shutting, you're not going to be in the mood for sex. I'm not saying you have to be wide-eyed and bushy-tailed to enjoy sex, but you do need a certain level of energy that sleepless nights may seriously deplete.

The good news is menopause lasts a limited period of time. At some point these symptoms will disappear on their own, and if they've been sapping your energy by keeping you awake, your energy level will rise when you can once again sleep through the night. But, since this period can last for quite some time, you shouldn't abandon your partner. I suggest you make some adjustments to your lovemaking schedule so you can still have sex, even if less frequently than before. Try to identify the times of day when you feel most alert and make appointments to have sex. For instance, mornings, when you should be somewhat refreshed by whatever sleep you managed to get, might be a good time. Also, see if you can integrate some naps into your daily schedule, and then make good use of the energy they provide with your partner.

Keeping the fires stoked

Finally, go ahead and have sex with your partner even if you don't have the energy or desire to have an orgasm. Women don't have to take an active role in sex, and while I wouldn't recommend this as a normal practice, during this limited period rather than leave your partner high and dry, I recommend having intercourse in such a way that your energy level isn't a factor. Of course if, as you begin to have sex, you get a second wind and suddenly feel aroused, then you should try to have an orgasm. But even if this doesn't happen, it's beneficial to prevent your spouse from being sexually frustrated. I'm not suggesting you do this as often as you had sex when you had plenty of energy, but don't stretch the time in between too far either. A sexless marriage can begin to tear at the foundations of the relationship, and if enough time goes by those tears might not be repairable.

Overactive bladder

Many women develop what is labeled an overactive bladder. It is estimated that almost 50 percent of women over the age of sixty-five report some problems in this area. When the condition is mild, it just means a few more visits to the toilet. In severe cases, a woman may become incontinent, making her afraid of even leaving the house.

The constant urge to urinate can take its toll on your sex life in many ways. Some women are afraid they will leak during sex and so avoid it. Others let it ruin their social life and end up becoming depressed, which, as we'll see in Chapter 6, can lead to diminished levels of arousal.

What is terrible about all of this is that it is often unnecessary. Many women believe having an overactive bladder is a normal part of the aging process and so do nothing about it. While it may be true that many older women have this problem, this doesn't mean your doctor can't be of help. There are medications, like Ditropan XL (oxybutynin chloride) that may help provide the control a woman is seeking. If you have this problem, don't assume you're stuck with it or be ashamed to talk to your doctor about it. Instead make a point of going to see your doctor to see what help he or she can offer.

Other medical issues

While bladder issues are relatively common among older women, there are many other potential medical problems that can impact a woman's sex life. These are medical conditions that affect a woman's organs in some way, often causing pain or other problems. Since I'm not a medical doctor, and since I don't want the power of suggestion to make you think any little ache or pain might be a sign of something more serious, I'm not going to give you a laundry list of these potential problems. Suffice to say, if you feel something is not right, go for a checkup. Don't allow yourself to fall into the trap of thinking a particular pain is "just old age." It might not be anything serious, but then again, it could be, and left untreated, it could get even more serious. Don't become a hypochondriac, but do go for regular checkups and do make a point of telling your doctor about anything different about your body. Let your doctor decide whether a particular symptom requires further investigation.

Of course women do have real medical problems such as endometriosis, in which part of the lining of the uterus gets misplaced and causes pain. Such problems can cause you to feel squeamish about your entire genital region. This in turn can cause you to feel negative about your entire femininity which, of course, will affect your desire for sex.

So the question is how to deal with this. If you've read up to here, you've already taken the most important step. Just by being aware that you might start feeling this way allows you to combat such feelings. If a period of time goes by and you find yourself unable to become aroused, you should be able to identify the culprit. Say to yourself, "Oh, it must be that condition I have that's making me feel averse to having sex." And what should you do about that? Have sex!

All of our appetites require triggers of some sort. I'm sure there have been times when you knew it was dinner time but just didn't feel hungry. Then you sat down at the table and ate as much as usual. Once you tasted the food, your palate awoke and your hunger returned. The very same thing happens with sex. Just because you don't feel aroused before starting to have sex doesn't mean that you won't soon become aroused once you are naked in bed with your partner, touching and kissing and being touched and kissed. You just have to sit down at the table, so to speak.

Certainly there are times when a particular medical problem causes you so much discomfort that you can't become aroused. I'm not talking about those times. I'm talking about the occasions when you feel basically all right, but your libido is in hiding for one reason or another. In these situations, my advice is to push aside the negative feelings you may be harboring towards having sex and give it a try. If it works out, you may end up feeling better overall.

Take advantage of your feminine wiles

Let me give you a little speech about feminine wiles. Though many women try to fight it, there's no question that aging affects your looks. Yes, women can disguise some of the changes that take place, but, when you take your clothes off in order to have sex, many of those camouflages vanish along with your wardrobe. Take heart, the situation is far from hopeless. Older women can make up for some of the physical changes by using the expertise they've acquired over the years. If you're with the same partner, he's someone you know quite well and this gives you a distinct advantage. But this advantage will only be yours to use if, like the brass ring at a carousel, you reach out and grab it. If you act like nothing has changed, you're literally throwing away a valuable tool.

I would advise you to take a little notebook and make an analysis of your partner and your relationship. Think about the hints that have been dropped or outright suggestions made. Examine how you have sex and what changes could take place. Read a book on sexual techniques and decide which positions you haven't tried that might be possible and enjoyable for the two of you. By having an examination like this by yourself, you can pick and choose what changes you feel would be manageable and which ones you might never be able to accept. I don't want anyone to feel pressured into performing a sex act they find unpleasant, but you also shouldn't adopt a knee-jerk reaction either. So give your sex life some careful study and try to spot some areas where changes might be possible.

Case History: Laura and Paul

While Paul had often hinted he was interested in having Paula give him oral sex during the first twenty-five years of their marriage, she'd rarely done it. They had a satisfactory sex life and since she didn't particularly want to perform this act, she'd skillfully avoided it. But from reading various magazines, Laura was aware that as a man gets older he needs physical stimulation to have an erection. And she'd also read that oral sex was a particularly good way of helping a partner to become erect. So when Paul was showing indications of having reached the state in his life when he needed some help from her, she decided to put whatever distaste she'd had about oral sex aside. Because it was her decision, she felt much more in control and soon learned to like the power it gave her over Paul. And he certainly didn't complain to be on the receiving end of ministrations that he'd been longing for.

True seduction

Now I know there are women who resent the fact that much about aging often hits them harder than it does men. There's no denying this is true, and since the advent of the drugs to compensate for erectile dysfunction, men have one less sign of aging to worry about. But while an older man's eyes may stray to younger women, that doesn't mean he actually prefers their company. In order to keep your man focused on you, you have to be proactive on several fronts, including making changes to your sex life, as I just discussed, but you also have to make your entire personality more appealing by putting your brain to work.

Tip:

I know it can be frustrating when he would prefer to watch some sporting event on TV rather than spend time with you. Your feminine wiles are useless if he's not paying attention. But resenting the time he spends watching a ball game is a waste of your time and energy. Instead be prepared to grab the moments you can. Find out ahead of time when the game starts and ends and get ready to spend some quality time before or after that. If you don't like to watch sports, do something you like to do when the game is on. You can't change a lifetime habit, but you can still interject activities that you enjoy and that will bring you together if you prepare for them. If you maintain a positive attitude, you can fully enjoy your hours together, rather than pouting and ending up with no quality time whatsoever.

I've found boredom is a lot more dangerous to a relationship than any other factor. By using your brain to make every day as interesting as possible, you can protect your relationship from the ravages of time. If you take your partner to spend an afternoon at a museum, where he can be stimulated by both the art and your company, you have a much better chance of getting him to make terrific love to you that night. On the other hand, if you spend the night glued to the TV in one room while he's off doing something else, perhaps even watching TV in another room, the connection just won't be there when you climb into bed together. So, while you must pay attention to your appearance, put just as much effort into sprucing up your relationship.

At this time of your life, there is probably more time available for the two of you to spend together. The kids are gone, and you're both probably working less hard than you did, either because of retirement or because you're not at a point in the business world where you're just starting out and have to burn the candle at both ends to make your niche. So if you have more time to spend together, put a little effort into doing just that.

And, while I can understand since I'm a doting grandmother myself, don't substitute grandchildren for your children. Yes, you should spend time with grandchildren, but don't forget to save some time for yourselves. Those moments are absolutely necessary to protecting your love life.

Let's face it, you can't stop Father Time from marching on. The best you can do is to adapt to the changes the passing years bring. Just as you can only do so much to fight, say, a heart condition, there's also just so much you can do to keep your relationship healthy. But if you do nothing, your relationship will suffer, and so will you.

There are other health issues I haven't raised here, as they apply to both sexes and are in Chapter 4. The next chapter deals with the health issues that relate to men, but you women should definitely invest the time to read it, because, if something is affecting your man's sexuality, it's affecting yours too.

The Physical Changes
Men Can Expect
(Women: Don't Skip this Chapter)

Throughout mankind's history, as men would age it was common knowledge their hair would thin and turn gray, their paunches would grow, and they'd have problems with their erections. Now this last universal truth is becoming less of a factor, thanks to Viagra and the other drugs presently on the market that deal with erectile dysfunction (ED). But while the nature of the problem older men have with their erections is changing, the overall subject of ED isn't disappearing, because now there are other issues couples have to cope with that didn't exist before these drugs arrived on the scene. But before I cover this end of the topic, let me go over the changes men can expect before they need to consider the possibility of taking any drugs for ED.

I mentioned these changes in Chapter 1, but it's important enough to state again, especially in greater detail, not just for the impact these changes can have on males, but also because of the impact on their spouses.

The loss of psychogenic erections

When a young male goes through puberty and his hormones

kick in, erections are a constant companion. It takes very little for a young male's penis to become erect, and certainly erotic thoughts or sexy images will have this effect. Such erections are called psychogenic erections because they don't require any physical stimulation to the penis but occur when the brain is stimulated. As a man ages, these erections will become less frequent. At some point, every man will cease to have psychogenic erections altogether. Please be careful, I'm not saying he won't be able to have erections, just not psychogenic erections. When he reaches the point where psychogenic erections no longer occur, he will need physical stimulation in order to have an erection.

What every man who hasn't gone through this stage is now saying to himself is, "When will this happen to me?" The answer is, there is no set age. It can happen as early as a man's forties, becomes more likely in his fifties, and is almost sure to take place before he gets out of the sixties. As you can see, this is a broad age range. But long before a man can no longer get psychogenic erections, he will notice that he gets many fewer of them. He'll also notice that his orgasms aren't quite as strong, that he ejaculates less volume than when he was younger and that it takes him longer to have an erection after he has ejaculated than before—days, perhaps, instead of the minutes it took when he was eighteen.

This is all part of the normal process of aging and shouldn't affect his sex life very much, because with a little physical stimulation he'll still be able to have an erection and ejaculate even if he finds the time interval between such events needs to be a bit longer than when he was younger. And there is often a silver lining to all of this, which is that men who used to have problems controlling when they would ejaculate, that is, suffered from premature ejaculation, will develop more control than they ever had.

Case History: Ken and Eileen

Ken had always been proud of his penis, which was a bit larger than the norm when erect. When he would get an erection, he often would show it to his wife and that, in turn, would lead to their having sex. When he hit sixty, it became obvious to Ken that he wasn't getting many erections any more. And if he didn't have an erection, he figured he couldn't have sex. His wife, Eileen, was hurt by the fact that their sex life had plunged from several times a week to once or twice a month. She didn't know what to think, though she blamed herself, and this lowered her feelings of self-esteem, which had already taken a hit from the onset of menopause. They both became rather edgy toward each other, carping more than they used to, though both were unsure of what exactly was going on.

The most serious difficulty that can arise from these changes is how the couple reacts to them. If both halves of the couple are not expecting these changes to occur, then either one, or both of them, may misconstrue the meaning of what is taking place. He may think he's not as attracted to his wife as he was before and she may come to the same conclusion or assume an even worse scenario, that he is having sex with somebody else.

Do such reactions happen? All the time. Some men go off and look for a younger woman, figuring that's the only way they'll be able to have a sex life, while some of the women, as confused as the men about this turn of events, stop having any sort of physical contact with their husband without telling him why, which, of course, exacerbates the problem and can lead to the end of the marriage.

If both partners know to expect the change in his ability to have psychogenic erections, it's quite easy to adapt to it. They just have to accept that when they want to have sex she needs to give some physical stimulation to his penis for him to have an erection. She shouldn't resent this new duty, because it has nothing to do with her sexiness, and additionally it will increase their overall level of intimacy, from which she will benefit. This increased intimacy is almost certainly going to make sex better for the two of them. His need for foreplay may make him better appreciate her need for foreplay and, if they're both aiming for the same goal, getting the other completely aroused for sex, this can be very helpful to their sex life.

Tip:

When a penis becomes erect, it becomes engorged with blood. That blood is fresh, fully oxygenated blood and is good for the penis. Having erections are very important to the health of a man's penis. Young men have erections all the time, but when older men stop getting psychogenic erections, they may wind up with far fewer erections than is good for the health of their penis. And, in fact, the more erections a man has, the more erections he is capable of having, before needing to resort to a Viagra-like drug. So both partners, to promote the proper health of his penis, should make sure he continues to get erections regularly. These erections don't have to lead to intercourse necessarily, as the many erections he used to have every day didn't. They're just recommended for good health.

Bring on the pills?

Are one of the pills, Viagra, Levitra, or Cialis, an alternative for loss of psychogenic erections? At this particular stage, not really, because the problem is not one of erectile dysfunction but rather one of communication. It's not that he can't have an erection, it's just that he needs some physical stimulation to get it. It's a lot more convenient to physically stimulate his penis than to have him take a pill and wait for the proper reaction. Of course as he continues to age, he may need to take one of these pills, though they too bring with them the risk of miscommunication between husband and wife. But, at this stage in his life, all he needs is some sexy ministrations of his partner, which to my mind is far better than swallowing a pill.

Erectile dysfunction

As we examine men in an even older population, we find some of them progress to the point where erections are impossible, even with physical stimulation, or they can get an erection, but it isn't hard enough to allow penetration, or it doesn't last long enough for intercourse to take place. Again there is no particular age when this will happen, and for many men it may never happen. According to *The International Journal of Impotence Research*, studies indicate the number of men from age forty to seventy with erectile difficulties is in the 5 percent to 20 percent range. For most men, it will begin slowly, so that at times they'll be able to have erections, but the frequency will decrease more and more until one day they become impossible.

Male menopause

Some people speak or write about something called "male menopause," but the comparison is not justified. Every woman goes through menopause, and we know exactly what causes it and what happens. But while every man will undergo some changes, the extent of those changes will differ. And while a diminished level of hormones does play a part in some of the physical changes a man may undergo, the psychosexual factors are as likely to play a role in any diminished sexual interest or performance among older men. For example, if a man fears he might not be able to obtain an erection, he'll avoid having sex with his partner, and the less often they have sex, the less his interest in having sex will be.

📌 Tip:

The reason a man gets an erection is that blood is pumped into the penis where it is trapped. If a man cannot have erections, it could be an indication that something is wrong with his cardiovascular system. In fact, ED may be an early warning sign of other future health problems. So please, if you are having difficulties obtaining or maintaining erections, don't be so embarrassed that you fail to tell your doctor. If you need further incentive to speak up, take into consideration that perhaps by getting quick attention to the underlying problem, you may be able to correct the ED problem without the need for any pills, not to mention heading off further complications, like a heart attack.

Consult a doctor

If you're having problems either obtaining or maintaining an erection and think you may be a candidate for one of these pills, make an appointment to see your family doctor or a urologist, the type of doctor who specializes in this area. Seeing a doctor won't guarantee you get a prescription for one of these pills because men who have heart or circulatory difficulties should not take them. (Viagra was actually created to help people with angina, but when they discovered this amazing side effect, they quickly switched its marketing campaign. However because of its effects on the heart, your doctor must be the one to decide whether or not these types of drugs are right for you.)

I should point out that erectile dysfunction is more likely to occur in men who smoke, drink too much alcohol, are overweight, or are couch potatoes. So if a doctor can convince a man to change some of these habits, not only will he increase his ability to have erections, but he'll also be improving his overall health. I realize we live in an age when many people would prefer to pop a pill than put effort into improving their health, but in the long run, the added trouble will yield better and longer-term results.

 **Tip:**

I know there are plenty of men who order these pills on the Internet and never see a doctor. This is especially true of younger men who don't have a problem but think of these pills as insurance when dating someone new. What are the reasons you shouldn't do this? One I just mentioned: If you have heart condition, taking one of these drugs could actually be life threatening. But another reason is also important, which is that sometimes difficulties getting erections is a sign of some other disease, such as diabetes. If you go to a doctor for erectile difficulties, you'll be checked for other possible causes, and this could literally save your life. But when you order on the Internet, you're on your own. If your doctor has given you the okay and you can buy the pills on the Internet for less, well that's your decision, though I must warn you that I've heard of scams where you pay your money and don't get anything for it. But, if you don't have your doctor's okay, don't order any of these pills illicitly. The price you end up paying could be far higher than you bargained for.

Case History: Veronica and Jack

It had become all too obvious to Jack that he was having serious problems with his erections. Even if his wife, Veronica, was able to give him an erection through oral sex, it was taking longer and longer for his penis to become fully erect and more than half the time he lost the erection before he had an orgasm. Without telling his wife, he went to see his doctor and obtained a prescription for Viagra.

That night he took one of the pills, waited a bit, and then stroked his penis a few times and got a very powerful erection. He rushed into the bedroom where Veronica was on the bed, with her laptop open and surrounded by papers. "Look what I've got for you," he almost shouted. To Veronica, who had an early morning flight out for an important business trip, stopping the work she was doing to have sex was the last thing she had time for. When she started to turn him down, he grew upset and told her what he'd done. This only made her more upset, and he ended up masturbating and sleeping on the couch.

As with Veronica and Jack, when Viagra first came out, it had some unintended side effects with regard to the relationship of many husbands and wives. If a couple didn't communicate about the timing of his taking one of those little blue pills and, after taking one, he surprised her with both an erection and expectations, this surprise would often make her angry instead of aroused. Today, one of the pills, Cialis, is advertised as lasting longer, up to thirty-six hours, so there's not so much pressure on a couple to have sex within a short window of time. Yet, from what I've read, different men have varying degrees of success with each of these pills, so it's hard to say if you can count on Cialis as being the right one for you. They all have side effects, which can include headaches, flushing, and a stuffy nose. Since every man will react to each one of these pills at least slightly differently, and some men find one pill or the other provides a harder and more lasting erection, there's no telling in advance which one might be the best for you. If you're a candidate, I would suggest you try all three so you can discover for yourself which one of them becomes your favorite.

But even if the issue of time pressure is less severe than it was when Viagra first came out, these pills can still cause problems in a relationship. One is that if a man starts taking one of these pills, making him feel like a teenager again, his wife won't have made the same emotional transformation. Their sex life may have been tapering off, and while that's not a good thing, he can't expect her to suddenly ratchet up their sex life just because he's taking a pill. Pressure is pressure, and it can often cause the reverse of the desired effect, so, even if she does want to have sex more often, if she feels pressured into it, it is less likely she'll want to.

And, of course, there are the women we've talked about who were happy their men couldn't have erections. They'd never enjoyed sex and were unlikely to in the future, so putting an end to this part of their relationship was something they were looking forward to. As far as these women are concerned, their husbands shouldn't be messing around with Mother Nature by taking pills. Some in this group will continue to have sex unwillingly while others will say to their husbands, "I don't want to have sex, so stop taking those pills and leave me alone."

If you find yourself in a relationship like this, the time has come to make repairs to your relationship, as this is not totally a sexual issue but has larger repercussions. My guess is that you will need some professional intervention, because it's probably not in your capacity to fix it by yourself at this stage.

Another potential problem arises if she feels that because of his renewed manhood he's going to be tempted to cheat on her. I'm sure some men, when they fill their first prescription, do think about sowing their wild oats as they may have when they were younger, though thinking about it doesn't mean they'll act on it. But if she's afraid he might, this fear can cause a problem in their relationship. And, of course, if he goes ahead and has a fling or two, well, that can very well shatter it.

Of course there are also men who never particularly liked having sex with their wives, usually because of underlying relationship problems, and who were looking forward to the day when they could stop. In these cases it may be the wife who is pushing him to get a prescription, and the resulting conflict, though created by a reversal of roles, might have the same miserable result.

For couples who start out with a basically healthy relationship, the key to avoiding such problems is to talk about how you're going to integrate these pills into your love life beforehand. The planning the pills require may remove a degree of spontaneity but that's not the end of world. If the woman feels she is a full partner in the decision making, she's going to feel a lot less anxious about this whole new development.

And, if the truth be told, the man is going to feel better about it too, because no man likes being turned down, especially when a pill is influencing his penis. The alternative, as we've discussed, that he takes the pill without letting his partner know and then pressures her for sex, is likely to be damaging to their relationship, in the short run and in the long run.

If a couple is experiencing significant relationship problems, and they needn't just be in the sexual arena, I strongly recommend they see a marital or relationship counselor before resorting to medication to improve his erections. Otherwise the added pressure brought on by these pills could become the proverbial straw that breaks the back of their relationship.

All said, the pills can be wonderful

Although I've been giving you information on the down side of these pills, I don't want to give you the impression that I'm against them, because, quite to the contrary, I think they're a wonderful advancement. They've allowed millions of men who were no longer able to have intercourse to once again have a fairly normal sex life with their partner. It's not that they're going to have psychogenic erections each time they see a pretty woman walk by, but when the need arises, they can take one of these pills, and given the proper erotic stimulation, which may be only visual but could also require some physical stimulation, they'll have quite a respectable erection.

Psychologically based erectile dysfunction

As I said earlier, the number of men who suffer from physically based erectile dysfunction is relatively small, even in older men, and not every one of these needs or is able to take a pill. There are many men who have a problem with their erections that is not physical at all but which stems from some psychological issue. These men would improve their sexual functioning a lot more effectively using sex therapy than pills, because, while a pill may give a man the ability to have an erection, he still has to have the desire. If a man is having difficulty getting excited, these pills won't have the effect he's hoping they will.

In some cases, there are men who have both problems, a psychological one and a physical one. Until the psychological one is cleared up, there's no way of telling whether the pills could be beneficial in fixing his physical problem.

When a patient comes to see me, I do what is called a sexual status exam, similar to what a doctor does when you first go to her office.

I ask a lot of questions to see exactly what is going on in his or her sex life. Before you decide whether or not you should be taking a pill for ED, I suggest you do a three-part sexual status exam of yourself.

1. Determine the status of your ability to have erections. Can you easily have a psychogenic erection? Does it happen from time to time? Can you have an erection with physical stimulation? Can you give yourself an erection when masturbating? If you experience erections in these ways, it is unlikely you need a pill.

Be honest with yourself. Pretending your sexual equipment is in better working order than it actually is will only delay arriving at a solution.

2. Talk with your partner about your sex life and the state of your erections. See if your partner has noticed any changes. Determine how much your partner is willing to help, if there is a problem. For example, is oral sex a possibility? Find out what your partner's attitude is toward your trying Viagra or one of the similar medications. This part of the exam is very important because, in communicating with your partner, you might discover the cure to your problem without having to take the next step.

3. Go for a physical exam to discover if you are a candidate for one of these pills. Find out what the side effects may be. If you and your physician feel comfortable with your trying them out, ask for a free sample or a prescription for a few pills.

A word of caution is due here. Don't think that when you walk through that doctor's door your problem is automatically going to be solved. This could build you up for a large letdown.

What if you discover you are having erectile difficulties but don't meet the requirements for a pharmaceutical solution? Go back and make sure you've exhausted all the other opportunities for help. For example, let's say you and your wife get along, but you still have some issues. She might help you with your erections but she's not been overly enthusiastic about it. By doing everything in your power to make your relationship stronger, you may find she becomes more cooperative.

Since I've mentioned oral sex a few times already, you might be thinking that's what I'm talking about here. Yes, oral sex could be part of the solution, but it's not the only way a partner can help you— and you can help yourself. There's more on this subject coming in chapters 9, 10, and 11, so keep reading.

✒ Tip:

One way of testing whether or not the problem is physical is by testing for nocturnal erections. All men, including older men, have erections during the course of the night, usually during REM sleep, although that is not always the case with older men.

If a man is having erections while he sleeps but is having difficulties when he is awake, then the problem is psychologically based. One simple way of determining this is to use the "stamp" test. Several postage stamps that are still attached to one another are placed around the penis, and if the stamps are broken apart when the man wakes up, then it is likely an nocturnal erection broke them apart. If a man cannot tell whether or not he is having erections at night, he may be sent to a sleep lab where his penis will be wired up so that he gets a clear verdict.

Or let's suppose your doctor said you weren't physically capable of taking one of these pills but, if you made some life-style changes, if you ate better and exercised more, then perhaps in the future your health would improve to the point where you could take a pill. Making such life-style changes is guaranteed to change your life for the better in ways that have nothing to do with firmer erections, but often these changes take a team effort. It's hard when only one person is on a diet. And exercise can take time away from being together. So, if your partner is pulling for you, this could be an important factor. All the more reason to firm up your relationship as you firm up your erections.

And there's also the question of your partner's sexual satisfaction. Whatever solution you reach, there may be times when your ability to get erections is touch and go. If you want your partner to be as patient and cooperative as possible, it's up to you to make sure you give her an orgasm if she wants one. This will do wonders for your relationship and for your sex life.

Viagra alternatives

Of course there are men who cannot take one of these pills because of an underlying medical condition that is not going to soon disappear. Does this mean they can't get erections? There were treatments for ED before Viagra and those still exist.

Testosterone therapy

The main male sex hormone is called testosterone. As a man ages, he produces less and less of it. This starts about age fifty and on average a man will produce about 1 percent less per year. In addition, the usable testosterone is the so-called "free testosterone," and older men have even less of this type.

As I mentioned, there is no such thing as male menopause per se. This is because there is no point when the male body stops producing testosterone as there is with women whose ovaries cease to function. Yet, in men whose testosterone production becomes greatly reduced, many of the same symptoms women have may occur, including hot flashes, increased irritability, bone loss, inability to concentrate, and depression—and, on top of those, diminished sex drive.

Some people refer to this as "andropause," as the male sex hormones are referred to as androgens. But whatever you call it, when it happens, it is often best to deal with it both medically and psychologically. Since certain medical conditions can increase this effect, further lowering the production of testosterone, it is important to consult with your physician if you are experiencing this.

HRT, hormone replacement therapy, similar to the therapy women have been undergoing and which recently has caused so much confusion concerning its benefits and drawbacks, is an alternative for men too. There are pills, injections, gels, and patches that can be used to increase the amount of free testosterone in a man's bloodstream.

I'm sorry to have to chicken out here again, as I did with HRT for women, and not take a stand for or against HRT, but the subject is just too complicated for this book. First of all, there are potential dangers because too much testosterone can increase the risk of prostate cancer. And from everything I've read, no one is certain which is the best method of delivery. Again, the bottom line is that the risks have to be weighed against the benefits.

Most men continue to enjoy sex without having to take any extra hormones. And much of the fatigue caused by the dearth of hormones can be addressed with an afternoon nap. The decision on what to do depends on the individual and the advice he receives from his physician.

Caverject

Another option is an injection of a drug, alprostadil, sold under the brand name Caverject, that men administer to themselves by injecting it into their penises when they wish to have sex. This drug was around before Viagra and will help many men.

Obviously, most men would prefer to take a pill than inject themselves, but not only is this a potential option for men who can't use Viagra or its counterparts for medical reasons, there are also men who have stronger erections when using Caverject than any of the three brands of pills.

Mechanical options

For men who do not respond to any of these drugs, a group that may include men whose impotence is caused by either the removal of the prostate gland or from diabetes or who decide against them for some other reason such as the side effects, there are two mechanical options, penile implants and vacuum erection devices.

Penile implants are semirigid or expandable plastic cylinders that can be surgically implanted inside a man's penis. The semirigid rods do not change, so they are more difficult to conceal when not in use, though they do bend so it's not as if it's sticking straight out all the time. Other types of implants are not rigid and instead include a pump that moves a saline solution from a reservoir into a cylinder placed inside the penis. These implants have greatly improved in recent years. Some dexterity to operate the pump is required, but the top of the line models are completely hidden and offer erections that are as firm as natural erections while leaving the penis quite normal looking in the flaccid state.

While such devices can experience a mechanical failure, the vast majority of men using them report they are completely satisfied. The cost is more than taking a pill, ranging from $15,000 to $35,000. Though these costs are covered by most insurance plans, including Medicare, there may be some co-pay involved. The surgery required for the latest implants can be done in the doctor's office on an outpatient basis. There may be moderate discomfort for a time and you'll have to wait until the doctor gives you the green light before having sex.

In case you're wondering how having one of these devices will affect your sexual functioning, the answer is that it should remain the same. Your penis should be just as sensitive as it was before and you should be able to become sexually aroused, have an orgasm, and ejaculate, providing you haven't had prostate surgery. In such instances you can still have orgasms, but no fluid will be ejaculated. An implant will not restore your powers of orgasm and ejaculation to those of a young man, though the psychological benefit of being able to once again have intercourse should rejuvenate your enjoyment of sex. As I said, most men who undergo this procedure are happy with it, as are their partners, and many of those who aren't had set their expectations too high.

Vacuum erection devices consist of a pump attached to a plastic cylinder. The man places his penis into the cylinder. The pump may operate by battery or hand power. The pump is used to remove the air from the cylinder which increases the flow of blood into the penis, causing an erection. Tension rings are then placed at the base of the penis to reduce blood flow from it so the erection remains during intercourse. Aided by the tension ring, the erection will usually last about thirty minutes. Many men report this method is quite effective, though it can take a few weeks to get the hang of it. It is a relatively safe method that can be used by almost any man, except those who have Peyronie's Disease, which causes a bend in the penis that stops it from fitting into the plastic tube. These devices cost from $150 to $450 and do not require a prescription.

Of course vacuum devices take some time to work, and this takes away from the spontaneity of sex. If you are in a stable relationship, with a long-term partner, this shouldn't cause a problem because you'll be working together on this. Some men report they have problems ejaculating after having used the device. However, if a man can masturbate or engage in oral sex to get an erection that leads to ejaculation, a vacuum device would only be needed when he wanted to have intercourse with his partner for their combined pleasure.

Herbal remedies

I've been approached time after time by producers of herbal "remedies" for sexual problems with requests that I give their products my endorsement. I've turned down these offers despite the large sums of money offered. That should tell you where I stand with regard to these products. And checking around, there is no scientific data to back up their claims either, so it's not just my personal opinion. I understand that because the profit margins are less than for prescription drugs, the funding to test these herbs scientifically is not there. Maybe some of these herbs do offer benefits, and it would be sad if the public didn't know about them. On the other hand, they haven't been tested for side effects either, and my question to you, my readers, is, do you really want to be a guinea pig?

Overcoming embarrassment

We know, while not every man is going to suffer from ED, millions do and that there are remedies that would enable the vast majority of these men to be able to have intercourse. However, a large percentage of those afflicted with ED continue to suffer because of a totally different affliction, embarrassment. These men are too embarrassed to visit a doctor and explain their problem. So they suffer, avoiding having intercourse, and removing this source of pleasure from their lives while damaging their relationship with their partner.

I commended Senator Bob Dole for making those advertisements for Viagra, because I knew that seeing a respected national figure on television admitting to his problem would give courage to many men to seek treatment who otherwise would not have. Other national figures have agreed to do paid commercials for these products, and I approve of this. As there has been more and more publicity about ED, certainly a higher percentage of men suffering from this condition have gone to see their physician. But the numbers who remain too embarrassed continue to be far too high.

Let me offer these particular men some advice. First of all, you don't necessarily have to see the physician you normally go to, and who knows you and whom seeing might cause the most embarrassment. For some men, seeing a doctor they don't know may be a lot easier. Doctors who specialize in these problems are called urologists. Of course, if your health plan insists that to get such a visit covered you have to get your primary physician to okay it, this changes the equation somewhat. But perhaps if embarrassment is really a major hurdle for you, it would be better to simply pay for the visit to the urologist rather than not go at all if you'd have to get the okay from your regular physician.

Of course, at some later point you may have to reveal your use of one of these pills, as your doctor will need to know what medications you are on when prescribing one for something else. But, once you've overcome the first hurdle and gotten used to using the drug, this revelation may not be nearly as embarrassing.

Another suggestion I have to overcoming embarrassment is to make an appointment and then send a note to the doctor ahead of time detailing the problem. This way the note will be in your file and the doctor won't have to ask so many embarrassing questions. You'll still have to admit the problem, and whoever opens the mail will know, but the truth is that they don't really care. It's your embarrassment that's the problem, and if you find it easier to state your needs in writing than verbally, then go ahead. At least you'll have gotten over the biggest hump which is answering the doctor's very first question, "So what brings you to see me?" The doctor will already know the answer.

I would also recommend talking about the entire issue with your partner before you go for a visit. First of all, she may help you remember some details that would be helpful. And if you can talk about it with her, this will make it a little easier to talk about it with your doctor. If you're too embarrassed to talk to your partner, at least have some conversations with yourself so you have some of the answers down pat.

Other changes

Since men are very concerned about their ability to have an erection, and since the arrival of these new pills, my emphasis up to this point has been on erections. But there are two other parts of male sexuality that I want to address as well: orgasm and ejaculation.

As a man ages, it will take him longer to have an orgasm and the sensations during orgasm may not be quite as strong as before. But unless there is an underlying medical condition, men should be able to continue to have orgasms whatever the situation with their erections. In fact, many men who can't have erections at all, meaning they can't have intercourse, can still have an orgasm if their penis is stimulated manually or orally.

Some older men complain that even though they can have an erection, they can't have an orgasm. This problem is usually psychological in nature. Let's say a man was used to having an orgasm after, say, five minutes. After a few more minutes have gone by and he still hasn't had an orgasm, he begins to worry about whether or not he is ever going to have one. Those worries will insure that, for at least that sexual episode, he won't have one. And if he worries about this again the next time, it becomes a self-fulfilling prophecy.

For men facing this situation, the first thing they must do is go for a checkup to make sure that there is no underlying medical cause. Once that issue has been put aside, their job is to focus on having an orgasm. The simplest way might be to masturbate while looking at some erotic material. The erotica might provide the necessary stimulus, and not worrying about what his partner is thinking could make it easier to have an orgasm. Once his confidence is restored in his ability to have an orgasm, it should then be easier to have one with a partner. If worries should start to creep into his mind during intercourse, I would suggest he conjure up a sexual fantasy that he finds very arousing and concentrate on it.

As to ejaculation, older men tend to ejaculate less and less fluid. Some older men can have orgasms without ejaculating anything at all. While this can be disconcerting, the point of having sex at their age is not to reproduce but to enjoy the pleasure of sex, and as long as they experience the satisfaction of having an orgasm, they should not allow themselves to be concerned with how much fluid they actually ejaculate.

Problems men have with body image

Of course problems with the ability to obtain or maintain an erection is not the extent of the medical issues that can affect a man's sex life. I'll discuss some of the more general ones faced by both sexes like the pain of arthritis or the lack of desire caused by a heart problem in the next chapter. But there's another problem faced by both sexes that I want to deal with here because it's slightly different in men than in women.

The problem I'm referring to is body image. One big difference concerning body image is that men and women don't share the same equipment. And while there are changes in the appearance of a woman's genitals, they're not as visible as a man's.

Body image problems may stem from physical changes but they are psychological in nature. An older man's penis will not look as virile as it once did, and that's part of the problem. But as men age, they often put on weight, and that, believe it or not, ends up shortening a man's penis. The reason is, the penis you see is not the entire organ. In men of normal weight, about a third of the penis is buried underneath the skin. But the fatter a man gets, the less of the entire penis is exposed, and, if a man is very fat, not only will the exterior portion of his penis have shrunk significantly, making some sexual positions impossible, but his protruding belly may make matters even worse so he may not find any position that allows him to have intercourse.

The key to curing this double-edged difficulty is for him to lose weight, because then his belly will shrink, bringing him literally closer to his partner, and his penis will lengthen, as more of it sees the light of day. Losing weight will also give him more energy, thereby increasing his desire for sex. I talk more about how to lose weight in Chapter 6.

Of course if a man doesn't like what he sees in the mirror, regardless of whether these changes affect his actual performance, this can make him less likely to remove his clothes in front of his spouse and engage in sex. So body image issues are something to pay attention to as they can have serious consequences. Once you start getting yourself into shape, the boost to your ego can enhance the improvements to your sexual functioning, doubling the benefit.

The male ego

The changes growing older brings about can affect a man's ego in many ways. Everything from losing his hair to loss of muscle tone affects a man's confidence. But these are unavoidable and usually happen gradually so most men adapt to them without incurring too much psychological damage. But there are other types of blows to a man's ego that can have a more serious effect, especially on their desire for sex. One of the biggest of these has to do with the ability to generate income. A common side effect that occurs when a man loses his job is that he also loses his desire to have sex. Being able to provide the financial security for his family is an important psychological component of a man's ego, and when his ego gets deflated by the loss of a job, so does his desire for the manly act of sex.

Generally, unemployed older men fall into two groups. The first are those men who are of working age, but, because they've been with their company for so long that they've had a series of salary raises, they have become too expensive for the company to keep. (The drain they place on the company's health insurance provider may be another reason they become expendable.) These men are going to have a hard time finding another job that pays them what they were earning, and they know it. It's no wonder they think less of themselves. Being fired like this may be the first sign they are getting older, and this can be troublesome too. The other group of men are those who are retired. Retired people face unique challenges and opportunities. I'll get into their case more in Chapter 9, "The Pitfalls of Retirement."

So how does a man get his libido in shape again after such a shock? The most important thing he can do is to admit the problem, to himself and to his partner. If he pretends there is nothing wrong, that he just doesn't feel like having sex, night after night after night, he's going to drive a wedge between himself and his partner, making it even harder for them to resolve the problem. But if they talk about it, if he admits that the loss of his job is affecting his desire for sex and his partner is supportive, in most cases, the desire will return.

The other thing I suggest is for the couple to spend as much time as possible in physical contact, even if they are not having sex. Hugging, cuddling, kissing, and sleeping close to one another will be of great help in repairing this blow to his ego.

Because men often associate touching with sex, a man looking to avoid sex may pull away from any physical contact. Knowing that he's not rejecting her, but that he's feeling dejected due to the blow to his ego caused by his job loss, she should look for ways of establishing physical contact which won't make him think she's pressuring him into having sex. For example, if he's sitting on the couch watching TV, lie down and put your head in his lap. My guess is he won't be able to stop himself from stroking your hair a bit. Even such a minor gesture can go a long way toward fixing the problem. But, if you jump onto his lap, making it seem as if you're asking to start a sexual episode, he might push you aside. So, if you're getting rejected, try the subtle approach and see what happens.

If the man really pulls into his shell and after a month there's been no improvement, it's probably time for some psychotherapy. I realize that if the family income has been reduced, spending money on therapy might not seem like a good investment. But whether his job prospects are good or not, it's important to protect your relationship—important enough to go for a visit or two with a professional counselor. It won't cost that much.

As we've seen, there are a lot of potential reasons a man might stop having sex with his wife. It might be ignorance of how his body is supposed to work, it might be miscommunication, it might be diminished desire, it might be a body image problem. But whatever it is, if he hasn't completely lost his desire for sex, in order to find the sexual satisfaction he craves, he may turn to masturbation.

Judging from the amount of questions I get on this subject, via letters or on my iVillage message board, masturbation while viewing on-line erotica is becoming more and more of a factor among men of all ages. I deal with how and when this practice can become a threat to a couple's relationship in Chapter 8. If you suspect this may be a problem in your relationship, please read it.

4

Shared Health Problems

Some of the changes brought on by aging affect people of one sex, but not the other. Only women go through menopause and only men have a piece of equipment that can fail them in their favorite pursuit. These are normal parts of the aging process and inescapable if you live long enough. But as people get older there are many other health conditions both sexes may encounter which, while not directly related to sexual functioning, can have quite an impact on your sex life. And only one partner needs to have one of these conditions to have an effect on your lovemaking. Of course, both of you may have the same or separate conditions, multiplying the complications. On top of this, many relatively common medical conditions are treated with medications that often have a negative impact on sexual desire. Among those on the list are arthritis, heart disease, high blood pressure, cancer, depression, and diabetes.

Do these factors mean the end of your sex life? Not if you don't want them to. Before going into specifics, I want to mention a man I met many years ago who was a guest on my TV show. He was a quadriplegic, which you might think would have made sex impossible. But he was married and did enjoy sex with his wife, and, in fact, it was a very important part of their relationship. Obviously he and his wife weren't having sex the way most couples engage in it, but whatever difficulties they had encountered, they'd been able to get around. He is living proof that you can overcome almost any hurdles regarding sex that Mother Nature throws your way—if you put your mind to it.

✒ Tip:

I've already told you not to delay going to the doctor for a medical condition, because this might lead to making it worse. But there's another reason not to delay, and that's illustrated by the old saying "The brave man dies but once while the coward dies a thousand deaths." If every day you're worried about some condition, whatever it is, you're actually torturing yourself by staying away from the doctor. It probably won't go away by itself; you might as well go sooner rather than later so you can begin to feel better sooner.

Depression

I've stressed over and over, your mind is the key. Some mental conditions, such as Alzheimer's, are beyond your control. And the most common mental problem, depression, may also fall into that category when it is particularly severe. Depression is not a condition that only strikes those over fifty, but it does become more likely as you get older. Untreated, depression will have a strong negative impact on your level of arousal, and the more severe the depression, the less likely it will be that you will want to have sex with anybody, at any time.

Clinical depression is not a condition you can overcome on your own. I'm not talking about a spell of the blues caused by, for example, the loss of a loved one. A tragedy such as this may require a mourning period of a few weeks or months, but eventually you can climb out of this type of depression without assistance other than the comfort of family and friends. And most of us experience a down day from time to time, but it is when there is no apparent reason for an ongoing state of depression that you need medical help.

Ironically, some of the medications that relieve depression can have the side effect of lowering the libido. Sometimes by changing medications you can find one that effectively deals with your depression without putting a damper on your sex life. So if you or your partner is suffering from a chronic case of the blues, don't ignore it. Consult with your doctor right away. Sex aside, life is too short to go through it depressed.

Tip:

Let me again repeat that any prescription medication, but particularly those used to treat depression, can affect your libido. If you notice this particular side effect, don't stop taking your medication. Instead go back to your doctor and see what he or she recommends. Sometimes the fix is quite simple, because there may be another medication that is equally effective but doesn't have this particular side effect on you. Or the doctor may say it is acceptable to skip your medication on days when you have sex. Or you might be given a lower dose. There are a number of possible solutions, but don't experiment without your doctor's participation because you could end up doing more harm than good. And don't be ashamed to tell your doctor that a medication is affecting your sex life. A doctor's job is to insure side effects have as limited an impact on your quality of life as possible.

Case History: Bob and Patty

Though Bob had always been quite an athlete, and never stopped exercising or watching his weight, he had a genetic trait that caused him to have a heart attack at sixty-two. After undergoing treatment, he returned home. His doctor recommended waiting a month before resuming normal sexual activity. Bob was very much looking forward to having sex with his attractive wife, Patty, but when the appropriate time period had elapsed and he broached the subject, she passed, making some lame excuse. Bob tried again the next day and the day after that, and each time he was rebuffed. Finally he'd had enough and insisted Patty tell him what was wrong. She admitted she was terrified he would have another heart attack while they were having sex and this fear was completely turning her off. Bob assured her the doctor had told him there was no danger.

Because Patty hadn't been there for this discussion, her fears were based on ignorance. Bob had her call his cardiologist so she could hear it from his own mouth, After this call, they resumed sexual relations and both enjoyed the encounters, though admittedly Patty still had some trepidations for the first few weeks.

An ailing heart

While the heart is a symbol of your love for one another, in actuality your heart is a vital organ that keeps you alive. When you have heart problems, particularly something serious like a heart attack, it's going to affect your sex life. I'm often asked how many calories are burned during sex, a question I never answer because I think it is totally irrelevant. But the fact of the matter is, unless a couple is

When One Partner Is Out of Play for a While

Even a small health problem can affect your sex life. The person with the medical problem may not be in the mood for sex for months, but his or her partner will still have needs. The obvious answer to this type of situation is masturbation.

Now you certainly don't have to tell your partner you're headed off to masturbate, but if you're spending a lot of time together, it may be hard to find the privacy you need. That can be especially true for women who require more time to have an orgasm (and, if they use a vibrator, more privacy with regard to any noise it might make). But while I would recommend discretion, as you don't want to put any pressure on your partner, you also don't want to pretend you've lost your sexual urges. Eventually you hope to be having sex as a couple again and the sooner the better. So be discreet but not sexless.

If you are the one tied up for the time being, be considerate enough to give your partner whatever space he or she needs to be able to masturbate.

Of course it is very important in these cases to continue to touch one another. You should hug and kiss and cuddle and let each other know you love each other no matter what. If you stop such activities, in part because they won't lead to sex, you may do considerable damage to your relationship.

atypically athletic in their sexual activity, having sex, no matter how many calories are burnt up, should not put much of a strain on the heart. Yet, if one of you is worrying about it, such worries could put quite a damper on your sex life.

You should have been given specific instructions with regard to sex after having been diagnosed with a heart condition, but some doctors gloss over this question, either because they are too busy or too embarrassed. In the case of Bob and Patty, rather than sit the two of them down for this discussion, Bob's doctor had discussed sex when Patty wasn't around. Perhaps he was embarrassed discussing their sex life in front of the two of them. But don't allow any feelings of embarrassment, yours or the doctor's, to cause you to shy away from getting the answers to your questions.

If your cardiologist acts too busy or too "high and mighty," and his attitude is one of the reasons you don't want to ask your questions, have your family physician call the cardiologist with your questions. I may be belaboring the point, but don't allow any excuse to get in the way. Do whatever it takes to become fully informed on this issue. The alternative is to allow your fear of causing further damage to your or your spouse's heart to destroy your sex life. That's far too high a price to pay to avoid asking your doctor a few questions he is supposed to be trained to deal with.

♆ Tip:

I've read that in the vast majority of cases where someone has died of a heart attack while having sex, the sex was illicit. While this is no guarantee of anything, it should somewhat allay the fears of couples facing this issue.

The first time

One very important milestone is the first time you have sex after a heart attack or bypass surgery. No matter how much reassurance your doctor may have given you that it is safe, a person who has recently had problems with his or her heart is going to have trepidations with regard to any physical activity they try for the first time, including, for example, walking up a flight of stairs. That's why the first time sex is attempted is likely to be met with at least some anxiety. Now fear is not something that is conducive to becoming aroused. And if either the person with the heart condition or his or her partner is having problems getting aroused, this will make the whole episode even more complicated. The key to your first sexual episode after a heart attack or cardiovascular surgery is to take it slowly and gradually. Spend extra time caressing and holding each other. Agree ahead of time that if one partner wants to stop and try again another time this is okay. The important thing is to at least begin the process, even if you don't complete it the first time. And perhaps you might consider other positions than the ones you normally use. For example, patients who have had bypass surgery have to be careful of their chest incisions, so oral sex might be a better choice while they are still healing.

Other suggestions for having sex safely after one partner has had a heart attack is to be careful in deciding when to have sex. If the patient is under a lot of stress for some reason, perhaps it would be better not to engage in sex until this stressful situation has passed. If the patient is going to have to engage in some sort of strenuous activity, that is to say strenuous for his or her current state, it might not be wise not to engage in sex right before or after this activity. And you certainly should not have sex right after a heavy meal or having had more than one drink of alcohol, assuming the latter is even permitted.

High blood pressure

Of course before someone has an actual heart attack, they may have other health problems that are precursors to a heart attack, most typically, high blood pressure. There are many drugs that help people maintain a healthy blood pressure. These medications, as I've mentioned before, may have side effects, some of which have a negative impact on sexuality, either because they cause some physical change that results in a lower libido or fatigue or some psychological change, such as depression. None of these are conducive to good sexual functioning.

The pharmaceutical industry is aware that people don't want to lose their sex lives because they have high blood pressure, but at the same time doctors need to control their patients' blood pressure, and, to date, no drug is available that is completely free of negative side effects. Here again, since different people are affected in different ways by a particular drug, sometimes switching medications is the answer.

While today there is not much you can do about hereditary factors that contribute to high blood pressure, one way of avoiding or alleviating it is to change your life-style in order to reduce some of the factors that may be responsible for your high blood pressure in the first place. These things include being overweight, not getting enough exercise, and smoking cigarettes.

If you can, don't rely entirely on medications for high blood pressure. Try your hardest to make some life-style changes so your doctor can safely cut back your use of medications. Since these life-style changes are guaranteed to improve how you feel, and reducing your medication intake should lessen the impact the medication is having on your sex life, you'll be doubly rewarded for your efforts. However, don't cut back on your own and don't start an exercise program without checking with your doctor on how strenuous your program should be.

Stroke

A stroke may cause mild to severe problems, often including forgetfulness and paralysis to one degree or another. Yet strokes do not necessarily eliminate one's interest in sex. The unaffected portions of the body should be the focus of attention when making love. As with other challenges to one's sex life, the use of ingenuity, communication, and patience will be paramount in resuming your sex life.

The pain of arthritis

Arthritis is another disease that tends to strike older people more often than younger ones. Since arthritis is painful, and pain reduces the desire for sex, it is a disease that can play havoc with a couple's sex life, particularly if both partners are afflicted.

Most people who have arthritis have it in a localized area so only certain movements are difficult or painful. Often times, a simple pain reliever can keep the pain in check. Changing positions may help. For example, you may discover your arthritis makes one position too difficult but that other positions can take its place. When trying out new positions, be especially aware of positions that may be particularly painful or even dangerous. Arthritic hips, for instance, have to be carefully protected so you should not try any position that will cause you to bend at the hip more than 90 degrees.

It's important to have open communication when it comes to coping with arthritis because miscommunication can make the situation much worse when it comes to your love life. You have to tell each other what is painful and what is not. If one person continuously has pain during sex, he or she may avoid it. But if you talk about it and experiment to find positions that are the most comfortable for the two of you, your sex life should only be mildly impacted.

The importance of timing

Arthritis may make the timing of when you have sex more important than ever. A person suffering from arthritis may find certain times of the day worse than others. This means you would want to schedule lovemaking during one of the times arthritic pain was at its lowest ebb. That might not be the time you were used to having sex, but this may have to be one of the compromises that keeps your sex life going. Again, such adjustments can only take place if you talk openly about it.

Another reason to plan sex is to time the taking of your medication so the maximum pain relief comes at the time you plan to have sex. You might also want to make a warm bath or hot shower a central part of foreplay, as heat can alleviate the pain of arthritis in some people.

Another way water could play a part in dealing with arthritis is if you buy a waterbed. The principle behind waterbeds, that the body's weight is distributed evenly, can make it easier for people with arthritis to have sex. The even distribution of weight can reduce the pressure on any joints that are inflamed. And since waterbeds always have heaters incorporated into them, you may find the heat from the waterbed helps alleviate any joint pain. Making love under an electric blanket on a regular bed might also be helpful. If you have trouble sleeping on the waterbed and have an extra room, place the waterbed in the spare bedroom. If anybody asks you why you have a waterbed and a regular mattress, tell them it's none of their business.

You may also be able to use pillows to diminish pain. For example, if you have an arthritic knee, placing a pillow underneath it may make a certain position more comfortable. Keep some extra small pillows in the bedroom so you don't have to run around searching for one in the middle of love-making if arthritic pain suddenly flares up.

As with your other concerns, don't be afraid to speak with your doctor about how arthritis is affecting your sex life. Your doctor may be able to prescribe a medication that isn't appropriate for everyday use but is fine to use to alleviate your pain for short-duration events like making love.

Diabetes

Diabetes is a terrible disease when it is out of control as it can cause heart attacks, strokes, kidney failure and blindness, to name only a few of the complications that can result from this disease. Uncontrolled diabetes can cause the destruction of the nerves responsible for erection in men, and so many men with diabetes suffer from erectile dysfunction. What is particularly bad about impotency from diabetes is that the man may feel the desire to have sex but there is no possibility of sexual release because he can't have an erection.

Viagra and the other pills can help, but often people who suffer from severe diabetes also have cardiovascular problems caused by their diabetes, conditions which make taking a pill or other drug for ED contraindicated. A vacuum device may be more appropriate, although if there is too much cardiovascular damage, there might not be enough blood flow for even such a device to cause an erection.

Some people are afraid the exertion of having sex will trigger a hypoglycemic attack, a condition of weakness caused by too little sugar, and that fear will decrease their appetite for sex.

Women with diabetes may also suffer from a lower libido, though the effects are usually not as severe as in men. Vascular damage can cause vaginal dryness and women who have nerve damage may have increased difficulties having an orgasm. Diabetes may also cause a woman to become depressed, which will make it harder for her to become aroused. Nerve damage to a woman's sex organs due to diabetes may make arousal more difficult, causing less lubrication, making intercourse more difficult as well. Couples should be aware that a woman with this condition will need more stimulation in order to become aroused. The use of a lubricant will help with the dryness.

Certainly being as careful as possible when it comes to controlling your diabetes can help lower the negative effects that diabetes may cause to your sex life. So if you needed any more incentive to be careful, let this be it.

Cancer

As we all have observed, cancer strikes far too many people. Some cancers are treatable, so they may create only a temporary reversal in a couple's sex life, while others are much more severe. Both the disease and the treatment can wreak havoc on a couple's love life.

Some cancers impact directly on sexual functioning; the exact effect will depend on the severity of the symptoms. But one cancer that is far too common and can have a severe effect on a couple's sex life is breast cancer. With breast cancer, one problem stems from the woman's disfigurement if she loses one or both breasts. She will certainly feel less desirable, and her partner may feel the same way about her. While in general I am not in favor of cosmetic surgery, breast reconstruction is one form of this surgery that I do support. Though a woman's breasts are there for the production of milk, and therefore not useful to a postmenopausal woman, they have become so ingrained as objects of sexual attraction it is impossible to disconnect them from this function. A reconstructed breast may not look identical to the one it replaces, but it will serve its purpose. And if it allows a couple to resume their sex life more easily, then I say women should go ahead with it.

But what if breast reconstruction is not possible, for either medical reasons or because of cost factors? Does this mean a couple's sex life is doomed? Not at all, and most couples facing this situation do manage to overcome it. I'm not going to say it's easy, for either the woman or her husband, but luckily the sexual urge is normally fairly strong and so the incentive of having sexual release will usually serve to bring the two of them together.

How you approach the first couple of times is going to be important, but there is no one approach that will work best for every couple. Couples in this situation are going to have to decide for themselves how best to handle it. If both feel more comfortable keeping the lights out for a period of time until they get their sex life going again, then that's what they should do. If they feel they'd prefer to get over the hump of the appearance issue quickly, that's fine too.

If that does not happen, and either the woman or her husband just can't handle her appearance, the couple should consult a therapist who is familiar with this issue. Very often the resistance can be broken down, but it's the first step that is the hardest to take and a professional counselor can be very useful in this regard.

Of course not every case of breast cancer requires the removal of the breast, but just about every woman with breast cancer will undergo chemotherapy and radiation. The side effects of these treatments are likely to make the woman lose all desire for sex, which is to be expected. During that period, however, it is vital her partner continue to offer her physical contact in the form of hugs and caresses, both to help her psychologically and to pave the way to when they can resume having sex.

But the consequences of these treatments will stretch beyond the time when she is actively undergoing them. The noted sex therapist, Helen Singer Kaplan, under whom I trained and who died of breast cancer in 1995, said: "The potentially devastating sexual consequences of the adjuvant treatments for breast cancer have been virtually ignored." One side effect of radiation, for example, is vaginal dryness, such as that undergone by women after menopause. Unless a patient is forewarned about what may happen to her, resuming her sex life is going to be all that much more difficult.

There is help for women who have had breast cancer. Not every woman wants to ask for it, especially during the time of her treatment, but at some point I would strongly advise all breast cancer victims to speak with her medical team about issues of sexuality because trying to overcome the consequences of these treatments on her sex life without some guidance will be very difficult.

Dementia

Another condition that strikes older adults that I want to cover is dementia, which can range from mild forgetfulness all the way to Alzheimer's. Dementia can have several different effects on a person's libido. In some cases a person suffering from dementia loses all desire for sex, while others become hypersexual, which causes them to make unbecoming and forward gestures and demands of their spouse and sometimes any other person with whom they come into contact.

It's certainly sad when someone who appears healthy starts to lose control of his or her mind, but as there is rarely a cure, there is little that can be done about it. The impact on the person's spouse can be even more devastating, as that person's mind is clear and yet their sex life may effectively be over.

While someone who is suffering from dementia will be under medical care, as I said, there may be nothing much the medical world can do. But this doesn't mean their partner can't be helped. If you are having to deal with a partner who has dementia, particularly Alzheimer's, I would strongly recommend you go for counseling of two types. The first would be for you own emotional stability. The second is to see what type of help is available with regard to the care of the patient. Don't try to do it all yourself because there are agencies which exist to provide assistance, both with regard to home care as well as in an outside facility if needed. Your doctor or hospital can give the information on agencies to contact in your area.

To the extent medical science can help people with physical or mental problems, you should avail yourself of whatever treatment is available, both to restore your health or that of your partner, assuming you can afford the latest treatments, which I know is not always possible. But while doctors can perform many miracles, it is not a perfect science and therefore, in many instances, a particular illness is just too overpowering to allow a couple's sex life to continue. That is certainly quite sad for the person who is ill, one more burden for him or her to have to carry. But what about their partner? Does this illness mean they too have to be sexually frustrated? My answer is no. If you have a partner who cannot share sexual intimacy with you and yet you feel the need for sexual release, my advice is to masturbate.

If you masturbated before you got married or if you continued to masturbate during your marriage, this advice will be easy to follow. While most men have masturbated, that's not the case for every woman. This is a problem that affects older widows and divorcees, because as women grow older there are fewer and fewer available single men. So without resorting to masturbation, these women may have no opportunity to find release for their sexual desires. But at least a widow or divorcee has the opportunity to find a new partner, and sometimes this hope is all she needs. If you have a partner but he or she is too sick to have sex, you shouldn't be looking for a new sex partner. Under those circumstances, masturbation is the right solution.

I know masturbation may not be an option to some people because of their religious beliefs, though I'd like to point out that the Biblical story of Onan, on which most religious bans on masturbation are based, was not really about masturbation but rather the withdrawal method, the man pulling his penis out of the woman's vagina before ejaculating so as not to cause a pregnancy, thereby spilling his seed. However I am not here to cause anyone to go against the dictates of their religion, so if masturbation is not something you feel is right for you, for religious reasons or any other, by all means refrain from this activity. But for those of you who do not choose to follow such rules and who feel sexually frustrated and cannot engage in sexual relations with your partner, for whatever reason, masturbation is appropriate.

I often get letters from older, single women asking me where they can purchase a vibrator. I don't know if they really need a vibrator in order to have an orgasm or are just inexperienced with masturbation and think they do, but they are easily purchased from catalogues such as Eve's Garden or Good Vibrations. For some women, the strong sensations caused by a vibrator are the only means that work to give them orgasms. For women without an available partner at present but who may one day have one and who can have orgasms without a vibrator, I would urge some caution. A woman can get so used to those strong sensations that she can no longer have an orgasm without them. If at some point in the future she is going to once again have sex with a partner, this could be a problem.

Hearing loss

While a loss of hearing may not be as catastrophic as some of the other health concerns, it can definitely have an impact on a couple's relationship, particularly if left untreated. Walk down the street and you'll see many, many people wearing glasses, so there's not much of a stigma attached to problems with vision, particularly as they can begin from childhood. But a loss of hearing tends to be a condition that strikes those sixty and over. Since people are often unwilling to admit they've aged, rather than head for the doctor's office as at the first hint of a vision problem, many people delay going to the doctor for hearing loss as long as possible.

Of course hearing aids cost more than do glasses and it takes longer to adjust to them, so there's no instant gratification the way there is with glasses. But let's face it, the main reason people delay taking this step is because of vanity. Now I'm not against wanting to keep Father Time at bay, but in this case there's a cost that makes this particular trade-off a mistake.

Case History: Guy and Sue

Guy was sixty-two and his hearing had begun to deteriorate over two years ago. At this point, it was obvious to everyone that he needed a hearing aid; everyone but Guy that is. In conversations, he had to keep interrupting to ask people to repeat themselves. When watching television he would insist on keeping the volume so loud it made it uncomfortable for anyone else to be in the room. And he avoided using the telephone as much as possible, since he had serious difficulties hearing what the other party was saying.

His wife, Sue, had been begging him to see a doctor about his hearing but he'd stubbornly refused. This infuriated her because his hearing loss was having quite an impact on her life. Lifelong friends didn't want to go out to dinner with them because they were embarrassed having to shout so Guy could understand what they were saying. Invitations to parties stopped coming for the same reason. Their social life, which was very important to Sue, was in shambles, and all because of his stubbornness. Sue had become so resentful towards Guy that the idea of having sex with him had become repulsive to her, and that in turn had made their sex life grind to a halt. Sue was terrified of becoming totally isolated by her husband's deafness and was beginning to think she might have to file for a divorce, all because he wouldn't go for a hearing aid.

What I learned when speaking to Guy was that his grandfather had been nearly deaf, and at that time hearing aids couldn't do much for him. The main reason Guy didn't want to go to a doctor was that he was afraid of being told that there was no hope for him, so he preferred to just pretend the situation wasn't that bad. But while not every case of hearing loss can be cured, the makers of hearing aids have made great strides in both efficacy and size. I convinced Guy of how serious this situation was with regard to his relationship with Sue. She wouldn't be so upset if she knew there was no cure, but by not agreeing to investigate possible solutions, he was exasperating her. He agreed to see a doctor and he was able to get the help they, as a couple, needed so badly.

Their case was a satisfying one, but one of the drawbacks of being in any of the helping professions is you constantly see people with a problem. In my specialty, people who have a great, or even average sex life or relationship never come through the doors of my office. That's why I have to remind myself from time to time that the whole world is not burdened by sexual problems. After reading this chapter, as well as the two before it, you might be left with the impression that even if your present sex life is okay, the future looks bleak. I want to dissuade you of this, because if you expect problems, you will probably encounter them. Some of you will face certain problems with your sex life, and this book was written to help you. In order not to miss too many possibilities, I had to list a good deal of the potholes that might await you. But just because they're out there doesn't mean you will hit any of them. And even if you do step into a pothole, that doesn't mean that your sex life or relationship won't recover. So, rather than end this chapter feeling bad, I want you to look at all this information as basically hopeful, because in the last decade or two we've made tremendous advances. And I expect that as more baby boomers hit the older age brackets where they might need help with their sex lives, it will be there for them.

5

Physical Fitness

As I've previously mentioned, one factor that can reduce your ability to enjoy sex is being overweight and out of shape. Of the two, being out of shape can have a stronger negative effect, because to keep a sex life from going stale, you have to inject a little stamina into it, which is hard to do if you're always huffing and puffing.

With so many Americans reported to be out of shape and overweight, it's obviously not easy for those of us who live in countries with thriving economies to resist the temptation presented by the cornucopia of good food that surrounds us or to pull ourselves away from the TV to get some exercise. I don't know if my telling you that dieting and exercise can improve your sex life will motivate you, but you must admit it's not a bad carrot to dangle in front of you.

I'm not a personal trainer, so please don't look to me for too much advice on exactly what you should be doing to drop those excess pounds and whip your body into shape. Nevertheless, I do have some words of wisdom I want to pass on that I think will be appropriate. Of course, please check with your doctor before starting any exercise routine, especially if you're very out of shape.

One of the factors that makes sex so pleasurable, beyond the physical sensation of having an orgasm, is the shared mental and physical experience. You can partake of some of that same satisfaction by dieting and exercising together. If the two of you work as a team, even if one of you needs more help in this area than the other, you'll be able to inspire each other to accomplish a lot more than if you were by yourself. Let me give you a few reasons weight loss done as a couple makes the process more tolerable.

Eat less together

If the two of you are trying to lose weight, menu planning will be a lot less complicated. But, if one person wants to reduce and the other is constantly stuffing himself or herself, meals can be a source of friction. If you both share the goal of losing weight, you'll both appreciate meals that are lower in calories and carbs. And if you can encourage each other each time you step on a scale, this enthusiasm will end up being a bit like foreplay—the calories you avoided in the dining room will end up having a stimulating effect in the bedroom.

Don't worry if your weight loss goals are different. Let's say you want to lose forty pounds and your husband only needs to lose ten. The odds are he's going to reach his goal sooner than you will. At that point, I suggest, rather than going back to eating the way he did before he started dieting, he continue to limit his intake so you don't feel deserted— at least when you're together. If he wants to eat a bit more when he's away from you or grab a snack when you're not looking, that would be appropriate as long as he doesn't start putting the pounds back on.

Exercise together

An integral part of getting into shape is exercise. It's difficult to burn off enough calories to make a dent in your overall weight, but if you can increase your metabolism through exercise your body will be burning more calories twenty-four hours a day, even when you're sleeping. And exercise will also get your blood flowing, which is very important to having good sex because the genital region requires extra blood to function, particularly in men; an erection is nothing more than a penis engorged with blood.

As with dieting, if you can make exercise time together time, it will motivate you and make the process a lot more palatable. Even a simple walk after dinner in the evening will be helpful to meeting your weight loss goal, and by going together you'll also get to share some quality time for conversation that will have an additional positive effect on your relationship.

If you're ready to progress to more strenuous exercises, you could take up a sport like tennis or squash to play together. Or go for jogs or bike rides as a duo. And by going to the gym together, even if you don't work out next to each other because you need different equipment, you'll be giving each other some needed encouragement just to get out the door, which many people find is the hardest step. And, when you get home, you can get out the tape measure and look for any progress in your various body parts. All that physical contact might be just the thing to get you to strip your clothes off and hit the shower together for a little bit more physical exercise.

I like to go kayaking, but I insist on using two-man kayaks so both paddlers can talk while they exercise. If you like to go bike riding, you may want to get a bicycle built for two. Skiing is a sport I also enjoy, but couples might end up going down different slopes depending on the degree of difficulty each can handle, but even if you are on the same slope, it's obviously a little hard to keep up a conversation as you're whizzing down a mountain side, so it doesn't really matter if you're not skiing in tandem. But when you're finished skiing for the day, you'll get back together at the lodge where you can share your stories of your best and worst runs over a glass of mulled wine, thus making it a shared experience in the end. And you can be sure the exhilaration you have experienced during the day will rub off later that night.

I'm not offering you a set of exact rules on how to work out together, but I am suggesting you do prod each other and encourage each other as much as possible so that you increase the odds of success.

Avoid competing

Of course there are some people who would hate the idea of exercising with their partner. These include very competitive people who have a chosen favorite sport or two and are only interested in winning, not spending time with their partner. To some extent, this is okay, but that person also has to be willing to make some compromises. If his or her partner is capable of doing no more than a vigorous walk, time should be set aside for them to go walking. Competing at sports is fun, but it can't replace all the potential free time you could be spending together, particularly these days when both halves of many couples work outside the home, and there is limited free time to begin with. The competitive athlete's body might benefit from engaging in his or her favorite sport alone, but the relationship will suffer.

Here I'd like to interject a word about one sport in particular, golf. Now if you both play golf, and you play together, that's great. But golf takes up a lot of time, and if one of you is a golfer and the other is not, golf can definitely interfere with your relationship. The person playing may be having a grand time, but the person back home could be miserable. They didn't invent the term "golf widow" for nothing.

I'm not saying golfers should give up their sport, but they also shouldn't act as if their partner isn't making a sacrifice. Playing golf isn't in the Constitution, so it has to be put in its proper place as a leisure time activity rather than placed on some pedestal as being more important than your relationship. If one of you plays regularly, I would suggest that you make up for it in other ways. For example, if there's rain in the forecast so you know you're not going to get on the course, get some tickets to a matinee or a museum, whatever activity your partner would enjoy, and escort your partner even if it's not your cup of tea. You have to keep in mind that your partner is making a sacrifice of time spent together every time you head off to play.

"But Dr. Ruth," I hear some of you golfers saying, "when I'm on the course, my spouse is free to do whatever he or she wants." If you both happen to be retired and have plenty of time in each other's company, then you have a point. But if your time as a couple is limited, regularly taking an entire weekend morning or afternoon away from your spouse is asking a lot. Again, I'm not saying you shouldn't play golf, but if you come back and spend the rest of the afternoon watching football or baseball and ignoring your spouse, then you've stepped way over the line. If you go out for a round of golf, you should show as much goodwill as possible by sharing some activity with your spouse.

As I said, I'm not a personal trainer, but let me offer another suggestion on how to make exercise more fun and sexy. When I said you should exercise together, I was talking about exercising next to one another for the most part, not actually doing exercises as a team. But there are exercises you can actually perform together, and by doing them as a team, they can also be quite sexy. The following are some sexy exercise ideas for you to share. Obviously if you're not physically ready for any of these, you shouldn't try them, and if you have doubts, ask your doctor.

The seesaw

Sit on the floor with your legs out and the soles of your feet touching each other. Grasp each other's hands or wrists. One of you lean backwards while the other goes forward, but providing enough resistance to keep you from falling all the way back. Then reverse the motion. If one of you has any difficulty supporting the weight of the other, let him or her know so that the person leaning backwards maintains enough muscle control so as not to put too much of a strain on the person doing the holding. This exercise needs to be done slowly, both to prevent injury and also so that you get the most exercise value out of it. In addition to the physical benefit, since the person leaning backwards is dependent on the one holding him or her up, this exercise helps to build intimacy as it gives physical evidence to your faith in one another.

Back to back lifts

This exercise may not be for every couple, definitely not for those with a bad back. And if your weight disparity is too large, it may not work. Just use some common sense before deciding whether or not to try it. Stand back to back and link arms. Taking turns, one of you leans forward, raising the other off the ground to whatever height is not too big a strain. Even if you can't lift your partner at all, just the effort of trying is good exercise.

As with the seesaw, the person being lifted off the ground will feel a bit nervous. By letting go and trusting their partner, added intimacy will result.

Couple crunches

Both of you lie down on the floor, put your legs straight up into the air, and then slide together so that your butts are up against each other, so that you look like an upside down T. (If you're naked, don't let the fact your genitals are touching be too distracting.) Then do crunches (half sit-ups).

How many crunches you can each do will depend on whether or not you normally do crunches. Start off with a low number and slowly work your way up.

Floor cycling

After you finish your crunches, push yourselves apart a few feet, line your feet up against each other, and push against each other using a pedaling motion. Don't try to do this quickly. Instead work to push against each other so you create resistance and give each other's leg muscles a workout. Here again, if one of you is much stronger than the other, that person will have to ease up a bit.

Hamstring burners

Exercises that work the backs of the thighs, the hamstring muscles, are hard to find, but not for couples that exercise as a team. Lie down on your stomach while your partner straddles you, facing your feet. Using his or her hands, your partner puts as much pressure on your ankles as needed to make it difficult for you to raise the lower half of your legs. As time goes by and each of you grows stronger, the "pusher" can exert increasing amounts of pressure. Eventually you should be able to do three sets of ten of these burners.

Wrestling

Now I'm not recommending you jump off the bed on top of each other or try to break a chair over each other's heads. That's not wrestling, that's fantasy TV. But if the two of you grapple and push each other around, with the stronger person holding back, you'll find you can get a pretty good workout. And if you do it in the nude, you may follow it up with another type of workout. Whatever you do, remember this type of wrestling is not a competitive sport. You're both trying to get some exercise, burning calories and building endurance. If you push, shove, and grapple with each other, you'll do exactly that and come away exhilarated. But if you try to hurt the other person, instead of a sexy exercise, it will be a mighty turn off.

Dancing

You might not think of dancing as a form of exercise, but you can certainly work up quite a sweat whirling around in each other's arms. Dancing is something you can do by yourselves at home in front of the stereo, or you can go out to some local club. You might even consider taking some lessons so you can add as much variety to your dance workouts as possible. If you don't want to spring for lessons given by a pro, there are also teach-yourself videos that will allow you to improve your skills without anyone else watching you trip over your two left feet while you're learning a new dance.

Bird watching

I was recently told that one of the fastest growing sports in America is bird watching. Now it's a bit of a stretch to call bird watching a sport, though if you're willing to hike off into the woods and carry a lot of equipment, it could have its aerobic side. But if the two of you aren't in good shape, at least this is one activity you can do together that won't be too taxing. And while you're scanning the treetops you'll be out in the fresh air having a good time. Even if your bodies aren't in much better shape when you return home, your relationship should have received a boost from sharing this pastime together. You can also fill out a journal where you keep track of the birds you've seen. It will give you a solid topic of conversation, talking about past birding expeditions and planning future ones.

Kegel exercises

In 1952, Dr. Arnold Kegel developed a set of exercises to help a woman regain control of her ability to urinate after giving birth by building up her vaginal muscles. After women started using the exercises, they discovered that they helped to increase the sensations they felt during intercourse. Once a woman had built up her vaginal muscles sufficiently, her partner would also gain some new sensations when she tightened those muscles around his penis during intercourse.

The muscles involved are called the pubococcygeus muscles, or more easily pronounced, pelvic floor muscles. To identify them, the next time you urinate, stop the flow. The muscle you use is the muscle you want to exercise. You should begin by squeezing it, then letting it go, doing five repetitions. As it gets stronger, you can hold each squeeze for a longer period of time and add more repetitions. You might begin with a half dozen repetitions and eventually get to twenty-five.

I would advise doing the Kegel exercises twice a day, at least until you've strengthened these muscles to their maximum, at which point you can cut down to three times a week, just to keep them in shape. If you do them at the same time every day, like when you get up and before you go to bed, you'll be more likely not to forget, though it can be fun doing them at random times with the realization that no one around you has any idea that you are exercising this particular set of muscles.

A woman with well-developed pelvic floor muscles will be able to give her husband's penis a squeeze he should enjoy. These exercises may also help any woman who has problems with incontinence, as that's why Dr. Kegel developed them in the first place. But Kegel exercises aren't only for women; men can benefit from doing them too.

A man uses the same exact muscle, which he identifies the same way, by stopping the flow while urinating. By building up this muscle, a man may find he can develop more control over his ability to ejaculate, which can be very helpful to men who suffer from premature ejaculation and their partners who suffer with them from too short episodes of intercourse. So, in both sexes, a prime beneficiary of stronger pelvic floor muscles will be their partner. Given those circumstances, doing these exercises at the same time makes a lot of sense.

Dr. Ruth's personal exercise tips

I've joined various gyms over the years, signed up for tennis lessons, and felt guilty about abandoning these efforts each and every time. My excuse was a busy schedule, but since so many people find excuses not to exercise, I'm sure that at least part of the reason I stopped going was that I was drawn into the I-Can't-Be-Bothered-Going Out-To-Exercise groove. And yet I think of myself as being in fairly good shape for someone seventy-six years old, and everyone tells me I have more energy than people one-fourth my age. So what's my secret exercise regime? I guess to call it a regime would be an exaggeration, so let's just call it my personal tips for staying in shape.

I spend a lot of time talking on the phone, and while this exercises my jaw muscle, that's not my tip. What I often do when I'm on the phone, however, is pace. It helps to have a portable phone, but even if I'm tied down by a phone cord, I'm usually walking back and forth. If you speak on the phone for an hour a day, get off of your duff and pace during those conversations and you'll probably end up walking a mile's worth every day.

I live in New York City, which enables me to walk a lot. So my second tip for all of you who live out in the suburbs is to move to a big city. This piece of advice may be problematic for some of you, but if you're contemplating a move, don't just pick a city for its climate; make sure there are sidewalks and places worth walking to.

Finally, when I use the word "walk" I'm not including in the definition words such as "stroll" or "amble." I go full steam ahead, sometimes so that my walking is closer to running than walking. When I'm at a convention, the people accompanying me often have a hard time keeping up, particularly because I use my small size to my advantage, scooting in and out of the crowds. When you set a good pace, not only do you get where you're going faster, but you also make walking more aerobic. So my third piece of advice to you is not only to walk, but pick up the pace.

The final Dr. Ruth tip concerns exercising your mind as well as your body. To do that you have to go out at night as much as possible. It's the opposite side of the coin of being a couch potato. If you go out as often as possible, you'll be getting a lot more exercise than you would be just sitting in front of the TV. Also, if you're out of the house, you'll be interacting with other people, and this will keep your mind in shape as well as your body. So if an invitation comes in the mail, don't look at it with dread, but instead look at it as an invitation to exercise your body, your mind, and your relationship.

6
Emotional Fitness

If you decide to get physically fit, developing a plan of action is relatively straightforward. I'm not saying it's easy to stick with a physical fitness plan, just that it's simple to come up with one. For example, you can go out and join a health club or just decide to go for a two-mile walk every morning. Do a little research and you'll find shelves full of books on the subject. And there are stores aplenty that will sell you exercise equipment. But what if you wanted to improve your emotional fitness? Would you know where to start? Probably not, and if you looked in the Yellow Pages, you wouldn't be much farther along.

Since, as the author of an advice book I'm not allowed to bring up rhetorical questions without answering them, this chapter is going to explain what you can do to tone your emotional fitness. Before you can begin making progress, you first have to assess your current level of emotional fitness. And when I use the word "your," I'm really talking about you as a couple, because to a certain degree, it's the partner with the lowest level of emotional fitness who has the most impact on your sex life. It's hard to soar to emotional heights if your partner refuses to even stand up.

So, what *is* the state of your relationship?

This is a subject where there are no objective measurements. If I ask you what the temperature is outside, you'd look at a thermometer and tell me the exact temperature. But there is no instrument to measure the temperature of your relationship. The answer is going to be subjective. One half of a couple might say the relationship is quite warm while the other might feel it's far too cold. But subjective measurements do have some value. Let me give you an example.

There's a good chance you have a thermostat where you live or work. And you know where a thermostat is set often causes problems because one person thinks the room is too cold while another feels it's too hot. So, while a thermometer can read, say, 68 degrees, 68 degrees will have a different meaning to two different people. You can't really put a number of "degrees" on your relationship, but you can, to one extent or another, quantify whether it is satisfying or not. You might rate it on a scale of one to ten. If you rate your relationship at an eight, and your partner does too, even if you're using different criteria, you've reached the same conclusion and your relationship is in pretty good shape. But if you rate it a two and your partner gives it an eight, you know it needs a good deal of adjustment.

Since nobody is perfect, I don't expect the two of you to rate your relationship at a ten. While eight or better is good, let's say one or both of you would rate it a five. In this case, I think you'll admit your relationship needs some work. You need to improve your emotional fitness.

At this point, if this were an article in some woman's magazine, I'd be asking you to fill out a questionnaire to figure out *exactly* what is wrong and *exactly* what you need to do to improve your relationship. I'm not going to do that because I don't think it's all that useful.

If the two of you can't find ways of improving your relationship in general, I think you need to see a therapist. (I'm going to talk at the end of this chapter about how a marital therapist or counselor can help and when it's appropriate to go to see one.) The advice I'm going to begin with, however, is similar to a weight-loss program.

If you watch any TV, you've seen advertisements for some gizmo that is supposed to flatten your stomach or take inches off your thighs. But the truth of the matter is that when you're trying to lose weight, you can't choose from which part of your body it's going to come. In other words, you can't spot diet. You have to lose weight in general, and different parts of your body will respond differently. I'm going to take the very same tack with regard to your emotional fitness. If you work at building up your relationship as a whole, somehow the parts that need the most work will improve, even without targeting them specifically.

So what's the first item on our program? It's very simple: Spend more time together. There are two important words in that sentence that need further defining, "more" and "together." Spending more time watching TV in the same room is not spending more time together. Going to the movies is, because you have to travel together to get to the movies, stand in line, and maybe you'll stop on the way home for ice cream or coffee over which you can talk about the movie.

One way you'll be able to tell that you haven't been spending enough time together is if, when you do set aside an hour of quiet time for each other, one or both of you has very little to say. If two people are good friends and talk all the time, they always have something to say to one another, even if they've just finished having a conversation. But picture two strangers in a room. The odds are there are going to be large gaps of embarrassing silence. That's because they have nothing in common and so they have very little to discuss.

Talk

If a couple has grown apart, no matter how long they've been sharing the same living space, when they finally do get together for some "quality" time there's going to be some awkwardness. If that happens to the two of you, it will just tell you that you need to be putting aside more time to be with each other without any distractions, that is, together, so communication becomes easier.

By the way, when I say communication, I don't necessarily mean pouring your heart out to the other person. Sometimes that's needed, absolutely, but good communication needs some back and forth. If one person is doing all the talking and the other can get by saying "there, there," then there's very little communicating going on.

If you haven't been communicating much of late, I would suggest you pick a topic that is somewhat emotionally neutral to begin with. No, not the weather, because how far can such a conversation go? But let's say one of you has a problem at work. Discussing what to do would be a good way of sharing your thoughts. Or maybe there was a good article in the paper or a magazine. Eventually the conversation has to get more personal, but at the beginning, you should be prepared with some possible topics so there are no awkward silences.

I want you to think of this process as "spring training," as when baseball teams first come together before the start of the season. When a team gathers its players at the start of a season, regardless of the sport, they're not going to be in synch. They need some time to train so they can get to know how they'll all react in certain situations. The more they work out as a team, the more cohesive they become. And the more the two of you talk, the easier communication will become. Once you've established a healthy level of communication about mundane matters, you can more easily talk about something serious. On the other hand, during the first few of these warm-up communication sessions, don't bring up sticky issues, because neither of you will be ready. Increase your ability to interact with each other step by step, so when a more difficult topic comes along, you'll both be better equipped to handle it.

Also, as you work toward better communication, you'll begin to feel more like a team instead of, perhaps, two competing individuals. Teams are supposed to work as a unit toward a common goal, winning the game. When the feeling of being a team has set in and a difficult topic comes along, your instincts will be to work together to come to a solution. In a relationship, the goal is to find a solution where you both win, not where one wins and the other loses.

I'm using a sports analogy here because very often (but not always) it's the men who have a harder time dealing with communication issues, so they may get a better understanding of what I'm getting at if I'm using terminology they're familiar with.

Men have been taught to keep their feelings to themselves but when they hit the boiling point, their adrenaline goes rushing up, and instead of communicating they may end up just shouting. (Of course women can have the same thing happen to them.) In other words, instead of communication, the result is combat. But the two of you aren't combatants, you're teammates. And you have to feel this way about one another. You have to want to help the other person, not want to win the argument. As every man knows, when teammates don't get along, they lose the game. When a bunch of superstars are on the field and their egos get in the way, the other team without the superstars, if it can play as a cohesive unit, can beat the pants off them. Just as in sports, in a loving relationship you have to push aside your ego. You have to try to come to a common solution and not score all the points yourself.

But ladies, you have to understand something about sports, too. First of all, this type of communicating is somewhat goal oriented. It's not about just telling your feelings and then feeling better because you got them out. If there's a man in this scenario, he's going to want to see that, together, you've made some progress. If you have some feelings rattling around inside you that can't be resolved, talk about them with a girlfriend or a therapist, at least in these beginning stages. Don't muddy the waters with all sorts of issues that aren't relevant.

And both of you have to remember that when the game is over, you shake hands and remain friends. If your partner has brought up a topic that upsets you, you have to forget about it afterwards. Holding grudges won't help the team.

Case Study: Alan and Selma

Alan and Selma had been married for twenty-seven years. When their kids were old enough to notice what their parents were doing, they would make a fuss when they saw their parents kissing or hugging, and rather than telling them to mind their own business or go into another room, Alan and Selma pretty much stopped giving public displays of affection. Even after their children had moved out, Alan would push away his wife when she got too close to him. He'd built up a habit over the years that he didn't stop to realize wasn't necessary or useful any longer.

Selma, however, thought it was because his feelings for her had changed. She'd put on some weight and he thought he was pushing her away because he didn't find her attractive, which was not the case. On their wedding anniversary, after he brought her a very nice gift, she broke down and cried, and this led to a conversation about the whole issue. Once he realized the pain his lack of affection was causing his wife, Alan made sure he hugged his wife at least once daily.

Touch

Returning to that word "together," you have to remember it's not only mental togetherness that counts, it also means together as in "close together," as in actually touching. (I used a sports analogy before, but your team is not a sports team. Touching, even in the shower, is not only allowed but encouraged.)

Some couples have sex together but rarely touch at other times. That's not a good state of affairs for a relationship. You have to hug, cuddle, kiss, and hold hands as much as possible. If necessary, set aside time for these activities. You can make this idea sound silly, "eight-thirty, time for hugging and kissing," but if you go for days without doing any of these activities, the idea isn't silly at all. For example, you could very easily set your alarm for five minutes earlier than usual and spend those five minutes in each other's arms. Nobody can honestly say losing five minutes of sleep is going to make a big difference in how tired or alert they feel for the rest of the day. I suggest you try it for a week. If this is a big problem for the two of you, see the section on going for therapy, later in this chapter.

"But wait a minute, Dr. Ruth, our schedules are really different and I get up more than an hour earlier than my spouse." I don't really buy this excuse, but I'll accept it as long as you plan on some other five-minute period and stick to it. If you're the one who always goes to bed first, before you go to bed, find your partner and hug for five minutes. If you can't find five minutes during the course of the day, I have to reiterate that it's time for therapy.

There are young couples with little kids—he works nights and she works days—they might well have difficulty finding five minutes a day. But if you're reading this particular book, it's likely you're well beyond that stage. Certainly your children don't need constant attention. And even if you do work separate shifts, there should still be some small window you could devote to getting close. If all you can think of are excuses as to why you can't do this, you've got a serious problem.

So now you're talking and touching regularly. At this point, if you weren't doing these things before, your level of emotional fitness should be much higher.

"Romance" is a verb

The next factor we have to deal with is romance. I'm certain all you women out there have an intuitive feel for what I mean by romance, but I'm not so sure about you men. Even men who know how to act romantic may not really feel what romance is all about. They have learned how to do it by rote, and while their partners appreciate their efforts, they do miss some of the depth.

Love is an emotion, and we've all felt it. I think I can say this with confidence about both the men and women reading this book. You men have looked at your partners and felt some sort of pang in your chest that you know as love. Of course the exhilarating feeling of walking on air you get when you are first dating tends to lessen after a while. At first your love soars but eventually it begins to descend. If it hits a certain plateau, this is fine. But sometimes rather than hitting a plateau, it continues to sink. So how do you keep it from sinking? How do you add some buoyancy to your love? The answer is by adding romance.

Picture a boat on a lake. If the level of the water goes down, the boat goes down with it until it hits bottom and can't float any more. Romance is the water in this lake. If you put some effort into pumping water into your personal lake, the boat holding your relationship will continue to float. But if you neglect to work at it, the lake will empty out and your relationship will settle into the mud.

When you take your partner's hand, when you bring home flowers, when you cook your partner's favorite meal, when you plan a vacation together, when you buy your partner a surprise gift, when you put your arms around your partner, when you tell your partner you love him or her, you're being romantic and pumping water into the lake.

I'm sure some of you men are saying to yourselves, practical guys that you are, where is the water going to? If there's a leak somewhere, let me find it and fix it. The problem is, the level of water isn't sinking because of a leak, it's going down because of evaporation. Every second, water molecules are rising because of the heat of your life. You're running around doing this and that, not concentrating on each other. All this activity causes enough heat to generate evaporation. Unless you stop, concentrate on each other, and pump some more water into your lake of love, your boat is going to hit rock bottom.

What constitutes water in our little metaphor? Romantic gestures. A romantic gesture is something you do for your partner specifically to show your love for him or her. Exactly what you do isn't that important, but it has to be directed at the other party. Taking out the garbage or ironing a shirt or changing a flat tire isn't romantic, not because it's not a selfless act, which it is, but because it's not a gesture of love. But if your partner is reading the paper and you peel an orange and set it down next to her, that's romantic. Your partner didn't need the orange. She might not have been thinking about it. But you knew she would enjoy it and without asking, you went and peeled the orange and put it on a plate and brought it to her.

There are some people who seem to believe the more you spend, the more romantic the gesture. I care to disagree. I'm not against receiving expensive gifts, mind you, but the price tag on a gift doesn't necessarily increase its romantic quotient. In fact, sometimes it's just the easy way out. And expensive gifts can sometimes backfire altogether. If the person giving expects a return of equal worth, or if the giver thinks that one or two such gestures a year will be enough, he or she is sorely mistaken. Romantic gestures have much more of an impact if served in regular, smaller doses. Love is a delicate emotion that needs to be misted daily rather than splashed with a giant wave once or twice a year.

So to be romantic is really very easy: All you have to do is think about your partner lovingly and let them know it, either verbally or through small gestures. If you spend a lot of time together and let each other know you love one another, you are being romantic. But if you steer clear of your partner most of the time and gripe about stuff when you are together, then you're being very unromantic.

Making love improves your emotional fitness

Is that all there is to an emotional relationship, to communicate, to cuddle, and to be romantic? If that's what you're thinking, then you're missing something. You also have to be sexy. I've got a whole chapter devoted to making your relationship more sexy, but I still want to make a few comments here about how being sexy boosts your emotional fitness.

Humans are sexual because it's part of procreation. But once you've passed the stage of making babies, there's no need to continue having sex. Or is there? I'm sure that you have good friends, of both sexes, with whom you like to spend time, talk, maybe even hug. So what sets off your various friendships from your one true love? Sexual attraction.

Now it's true humans can have casual sex, even with complete strangers. We all have this part of us called lust and it can be satisfied in different ways. But if you look around you, you know sex from lust isn't enough because most people do form couples. There is something special about making love to someone you love that is more satisfying than just having sex with someone with whom you are not in love. But guess what, if you remove making love from a relationship, it can be very damaging. Sex is one of the glues that hold the two of you together. I'm not saying couples who can't have sex can't stay together, as of course many who have a physical problem that prevents them from having sex do. But while two people might stick it out without sex, it does tear at the relationship. And if there is no physical excuse, those tears can quickly grow to major fractures that become irreparable.

Why do I even have to be talking about this subject? Because as you get older the sex drive diminishes and if you're slowly drifting apart sexually you could wind up so far apart that you can't come back together. Even if you remain together as a couple, you won't be the same couple you would be if you maintained sexual relations. And if one partner desires sex and the other refuses to have sexual relations, the frustrated partner is going to be angry, and life for the two of them could wind up being unpleasant. Such couples sometimes stay together because they need each other for other reasons, but the daily friction wears at them and makes their final years together full of bitterness rather than love.

If you're not able to get into physical shape by yourself, the best thing you can do is hire a personal trainer. While the trainer's knowledge is important, even more important is the fact that you have made a commitment the trainer will confront you with. This is a strong motivating factor to get you to actually follow the exercise program.

Going to see a marital or sex therapist has the same effect. It motivates you to confront and work on the problems you have.

How to judge if you need professional help

Have you ever gone to the doctor with a little ache, pain, or skin lesion that you thought could be a sign of something more serious and then left relieved that it was nothing? I think most of us have done that. This problem, whatever it was, was minor but it was bothering you and that's what drove you to consult a doctor.

There's this misconception that therapy has to go on forever. Once you step into a therapist's office you're going to be there for years. Now that may be true for psychoanalysis, but for someone like me, a sex therapist, that's not true at all.

I can see clients as little as one or two times and be very helpful. Of course different types of therapists need different amount of times. But still in all, therapy is not necessarily a type of treatment where you need to make a tremendous investment, either in terms of time or money. So if you have a relationship issue of some sort, you should understand that you can treat a therapist the way you treat a doctor. If the problem turns out to be minor, your treatment will also be minor.

The decision of when to see a therapist need not be a traumatic one. You don't have to feel that your relationship is about to fall apart. (And, sadly, when people wait until that stage, it's often too late to fix the problem.) If you feel that something is wrong and it is bothering you, even if it feels like something minor, you should consider the idea of seeing a therapist or counselor.

If the issue has grown to the point where you are losing sleep over it, are fighting continually with your partner, wonder whether you belong together, find yourself crying or looking at other people, then you've reached a stage where it's no longer a question of whether or not, but how soon you need to make that appointment. And in my estimation, the sooner the better; like today!

Making the best use of therapy

Fixing the problem isn't always the hardest part of becoming emotionally fit. More often than not it's taking the first step of admitting there are problems. Going to see a therapist sends this message in a loud and clear voice—to yourself if to no one else.

The other thing a therapist offers is the ability to act as a referee. A therapist will usually talk to each of you alone to get a picture of what is going on in the relationship. More often than not, each half of the couple will report a different perspective. Sometimes their views are like night and day. By knowing each partner's view of the situation, the therapist can begin to try to get their views to merge.

Most of the time I am successful at getting couples to resolve their differences, but sadly that's not always the case.

Stay in a marriage at any cost?

Some couples avoid going to therapy because deep down they fear this step will spell the beginning of the end of the relationship. Sometimes, once both partners admit to themselves how far apart they've drifted, the only fruitful outcome is to separate. Sometimes, when there are young children, it may be better to stick it out. But the readers of this book are past that point.

For an older woman, finding a new partner may be a challenge. Because men die sooner than women, the older a woman gets, the smaller the pool of available men. Because of these odds, should this woman stay in a marriage that has severe problems? I say the answer to that question is no.

Change can be a scary thing, I know, but most of the time when a woman, or a man, leaves an unhappy marriage, they find an enormous sense of relief. They may mourn the marriage for a month or two, but eventually the vast majority feel they made the right move. There may be difficulties in being alone, but all in all they don't compare to being made miserable day after day by a spouse.

In a later chapter I'm going to give single adults advice on how to find a new partner. So whatever the odds, just remember that all hope isn't lost.

Where to find a therapist

One question I'm often asked is how to go about finding a therapist. The answer to this question has gotten both easier and harder. How has it gotten easier? The Internet now offers plenty of directories so, even if you don't live in a large city where there are plenty to choose from, you can find one that is relatively nearby without searching through dozens of phone books. But the increase in the number of options can also make it harder to decide which one to choose.

Please see the "Resources" section at the end of this book for a list of organizations that can help you find a therapist near you. If you have access to the Internet, you can actually look them up on line. All of them have some sort of system to help you choose from the therapists in their directories. Of course just because someone is listed doesn't mean they're good. Some states give credentials far too easily. That's why you need to follow a few simple rules before making an appointment.

The first thing I would advise you to do is to ask around among your friends and family. Now it's true that people won't always readily admit they've gone for therapy, and you, also, may want to keep your need for therapy a secret. But if you say you're asking on the part of a friend, your friend or family member can tell you they've heard about a therapist from a another friend, and then you're both covered but you still get the information. Those types of white lies can be useful when dealing with this topic.

You can also ask your doctor, who may well have recommended other patients and so has been given useful feedback as to which counselors in the community are better than others. Your religious leader, who in some cases could do the counseling himself or herself, also may know of therapists who have been effective.

Next, when you do call a therapist, don't be intimidated. Make sure you ask a lot of questions such as what their credentials actually are, how long they've been practicing, and what percentage of their work involves people with your problem. You can also ask them how long they usually work with couples. I believe you should begin with short-term therapy so you can judge whether or not you're making progress.

If after a couple of sessions you feel your therapist is not working out, don't be afraid to stop going to this therapist, but also don't jump to the conclusion that therapy isn't for you. These days, people seek out a second opinion on all sorts of medical treatments because we've come to recognize that not every person in the helping professions is equal. In fact, it's quite all right to admit to a therapist that you intend to have a couple of sessions together before you make up your mind to stick with her. The chemistry between you and your therapist is an important factor in determining how successful this therapy is going to be. And when mental rather than physical issues are at play, your opinion of the health practitioner is going to be a lot more subjective. So be choosy, just don't be so choosy that you don't get the help you need.

Cost is, of course, another factor, but don't let it be the only one. If your health insurance provider gives you a list to choose from and they all turn out to be young and inexperienced, therefore willing to take the lower fees paid by some HMOs, give serious consideration to paying for this yourself. You might try one of these new therapists, but don't put all of your trust in them. Keep in mind that many therapists work on a sliding scale; if they quote you one price when you first ask, they may be willing to lower it if you let them know that the price will affect your decision of whether or not to use them. And, finally, social workers, who usually work at large, teaching hospitals, may offer the most affordable rates. If the social worker is well-trained and has a lot of experience, this route may offer the most cost-effective counseling you can get. Large hospitals also usually have a referral service, so that's another way to get a recommendation for an outside therapist.

For those of you without access to a computer, the American Psychological Association (call 1-800-964-2000) offers a free referral service. But keep in mind, even if you don't have your own computer hooked up to the Web, your local library has computers—and learning to use one is not complicated.

Spicing Up Your Love Life

As I said in the previous chapter, keeping your sex life active is an important part of making sure your relationship is in good shape. And since that's my particular area of expertise, I'm going to devote a chapter to this subject.

Now, since the readers of this book are on the older side, I have to lead off with a disclaimer, which is going to be very simple: Use your common sense. While I'm not going to recommend that anyone reading this book try to have sex while hanging from a chandelier, I will suggest, for example, that you make use of rooms other than the bedroom. But, if one or both of you have a fragile body part which requires you to be on a nice soft bed, then ignore my advice to experiment in the kitchen or bathroom where hard floors and counters rule.

Having gotten that out of the way, allow me to reiterate something I said earlier: The most important organ with regard to good sex is not your genitals, but your brain. Obviously your genitals have to be working properly, and, without your brain, you wouldn't be able to notice the pleasurable sensations your genitals are capable of producing. But the brain comes into play to a greater degree than simply reporting what is happening with your genitals. Therefore, keep this in mind: If you want to spice up your sex life, you have to use your noggin.

For your brain to be fully engaged, it mustn't always know ahead of time exactly what is going to happen. If you've developed a sex routine and you stick to it each and every time you have sex, your brain is going to get bored, and boredom is a sure killer of sexual enjoyment.

I'm not telling you not to have sexual routines. There are times when the tried and true are best because you don't have the energy for much else. But, if you venture out of your normal patterns once in a while, the buildup of sexual energy from these experiences can be banked and carried over for the times you're following your routine. If you follow the same routine each and every time you have sex, there's no surplus to use at other times.

While I'm certainly not going to tell you that, as an older adult, you should avoid consulting the *Kama Sutra*, let me start out with some basic things you can do to break up the routines you may have.

The first is to alternate who initiates sex. If one of you is always the one to make the first move, several problems may arise. The person doing the initiating is also the only one who gets turned down. Getting turned down always causes some negative feelings and even minor events of this sort can, over time, damage your relationship. The other partner, the one who never initiates sex, may be passing up opportunities for sexual pleasure when he or she is the most ready. Yes, this person may have to deal with getting turned down once in a while too, but if your relationship is healthy and you love each other, that's not such a big deal.

The value of intimacy

Only one of you always initiating the sex is also a sign of a lack of intimacy. It suggests one of you is afraid to let his or her hair down, so to speak, in front of the other. Asking to have sex makes one vulnerable, and vulnerability is an integral part of intimacy.

"Wait," I hear you protesting, "We have sex, so of course we're intimate."

When a man has sex with a prostitute, is that an intimate act? Of course it isn't. If a woman allows her partner to have intercourse with her, but never enjoys it, that's not being intimate either. So you can have sex that isn't truly intimate. What you want to cultivate is an atmosphere that is the opposite of these two situations. You want the sexual act you are engaging in to have as much love, caring, and sharing as possible, because that way it will give both of you the greatest pleasure. The only way for this to happen is if the two of you are being as intimate as possible. If one or both of you are holding back, for whatever reason, then you can't hit the sexual heights you desire.

When you were younger, your level of sexual desire may have been greater. This may have made it possible for you to have rewarding sex without a high level of intimacy. In fact, the very freshness that accompanies the first few times a couple makes love is what makes these particular acts of lovemaking special. But this newness wears off after a while, and then you have to substitute something else: intimacy.

Intimacy in a relationship can wax and wane. If you got married and had kids, some of the intimacy you were building up prior to becoming parents undoubtedly evaporated. As we talked about previously, kids take away from their parents' privacy and amount of free time, and this tends to push intimacy aside.

At this stage in your life, the kids, if there are any, have probably moved out, not to mention that they're no longer kids, so this shouldn't be a barrier to intimacy. Yet, your bodies have aged, and you could be letting body image concerns get in the way of intimacy. And, as we've seen, dealing with the changes brought on by menopause in women and the loss of psychogenic erections in men can actually increase your level of intimacy, while not dealing with them will have the opposite effect.

No matter where you fall on the intimacy continuum, a big step in livening up your sex life is to increase your level of intimacy.

Some strategies for increasing your intimacy

There's an exercise we sex therapists call body mapping. Each partner examines the other's naked body, trying to find their erogenous zones. He might rub, tickle, lick, nuzzle, and kiss various parts of her body from head to toe as she indicates to him how each touch or caress feels, either verbally or by making little (or perhaps big) groaning noises. She then would do the same to him.

The odds are this activity is going to get you both aroused and this arousal will lead to your having sex, but that's not the main goal. What you're looking to do is to make note of the parts of your partner's body—in addition to the ones you already know about—that cause him or her the greatest pleasure and to become more intimate in the process.

Another way to increase intimacy is to have sex very, very slowly, from start to finish—from taking off your clothes all the way to putting them back on, do everything as slowly as possible. Tantric sex, based on Eastern philosophies, champions this practice.

I'm not advocating that you slow your lovemaking to a crawl every time; I'm just saying that as an intimacy exercise, every once in a while, have sex extra slowly so you can concentrate on each sensation.

As part of this slow lovemaking, choose a position where you're sitting facing each other, either on a chair or in bed. The man should place his penis inside his partner, but both of you should resist the urge to thrust in and out. Just remain one inside the other, looking deeply into each other's eyes. Of course, in the end, you're both going to want to have orgasms, and you should do whatever is necessary to achieve them, but by the end of this extra slow encounter, I can guarantee your level of intimacy will have gone up a few notches.

Finally, I want you to go for a long walk someplace quiet and have a talk about your sex life. I'm not telling you to share your wild fantasies (although this might be a great conversation for another time), but to discuss the basics. Are you both satisfied with how often you're having sex, the manner in which you're doing it, the timing, the places, and so on? Please don't get into a fight over this. Just exchange views and, if you find areas one or the both of you would like to work on—as you most likely will—agree to make some changes that take into consideration what you've discussed.

If problems that surface during this conversation don't seem to be amenable to being ironed out by the two of you, consider going for counseling. I doubt any such issue is going to be simple, like one of you refusing to engage in a particular position, though some people do tussle over oral sex. Most likely it will be something more substantial like your appetite for sex. If one of you wants sex a lot more often than the other, this might be a sign of a more serious issue. For example, if one of you is angry at the other most of the time, this is going to affect your sex life. That's why I'm saying that in order to resolve some types of issues you may need the assistance of a professional, especially if a problem has been an ongoing one.

Another change you could make that might reinvigorate your sex life is to make love in the morning instead of at night. You'll recall that there's one scientific reason for this: Since the levels of the male sex hormone, testosterone, are highest in men in the morning, mornings might be the best time for him to make love. For most people, mornings are also the time when they are the least tired, so that's another reason for an occasional before-lunch love making session.

As I've been stressing in this chapter, nearly any change is good because it relieves boredom. If you're in the habit of making love in the morning, I would tell you to have sex in the evenings once in a while. And not always just before you're about to go to sleep, but sometimes earlier, even before dinner, just for variety's sake.

Case Study: Iris and Jeff

Iris and Jeff would routinely engage in sex only after retiring for the night. One afternoon when they were scheduled to meet another couple for dinner, Jeff suggested they make love just before leaving the house. Iris was a little apprehensive at first but eventually agreed to it. They both found knowing they would be meeting their friends so soon after making love exciting, and the sex was better than it had been in recent memory. All evening long they felt somewhat naughty with their secret and kept exchanging knowing glances. When they got home, they made love for the second time in one day, something they hadn't done in years.

I already said something about looking for new places to have sex, but let me expand. First of all, your bed is probably the only place where you have blankets and sheets, meaning where you can make love covered up. That's certainly fine in cold weather and cuddling in the cave made by the blankets is cozy and sexy, but it's also a nice feeling to have unrestricted air against your flesh. And, of course, it is easier to visually enjoy each other's bodies this way. If you're in a room other than the bedroom, there will be less temptation to cover up. If the house is a bit chilly, turn up the heat for an hour or so. I know this isn't supposed to be environmentally sound, but for the sake of your love life, I say it's fine. And if you're in a warmer clime where the air conditioning is going, turn it up so you won't get goose bumps when you're naked.

Bathrooms are a good place to have sex because they add the dimension of water. Bathrooms are also the most dangerous room in the house so you do have to be careful. But if you take the proper precautions, you can have a lot of good, clean fun (pun intended) in the bathroom.

Tip:

Washing each other is definitely one way of being intimate. It may also help with other concerns, especially with concerns about oral sex. There are many people who avoid oral sex because they feel their partner's genitals aren't clean. But, if you give your partner's penis or vagina a good bathing, not only will this be arousing to both of you, it will also allay fears about the area's cleanliness. (I'm not saying knowing a partner's penis or vagina is spiffy clean will always be enough to convince someone averse to oral sex to change his or her mind, but it's a possibility worth exploring.)

Another advantage of the bathroom is that it is an easy place to clean up. Sex can be a bit messy, and, while my advice is to ignore this aspect of it, if it really bothers you, having sex in the bathroom might be helpful to your overall enjoyment since you won't have to concern yourself with dirty sheets.

Tip:

If one or both of you are bothered by the mess inherent with intercourse, store a few towels under the bed and, when you're about to make love, put one underneath you. This will alleviate this particular concern. We certainly don't want your mind to be concerned with dirty linen when you're making love.

There are some people who like to be able to look at themselves or their partner while making love. Some people go to the extreme of putting a mirror over their bed, but bathrooms may offer an alternative since they're likely to have several well-placed mirrors. If you find you enjoy putting on a show for each other, it's easy to add mirrors to the bathroom without alerting visitors to their purpose the way a mirror over the bed would. Of course, if you want to place a mirror over your bed, please be my guest, but I do know it will set tongues wagging, especially when your children visit, so I can understand the reluctance of some to employ this particular sex appliance.

Another room of the house not usually thought of for sex but one which can add some interesting twists is the kitchen. Depending on the height of the individuals involved, counter tops can make sturdy platforms for having sex with one partner sitting and the other standing. A footstool might make this type of position easier—although more dangerous. Any tables and chairs in the kitchen might also allow you to experiment with different positions.

Don't overlook some cooking ingredients likely to be found in a kitchen, such as honey, whipped cream, chocolate sauce, or peanut butter. These can be used as sensory aids for culinary lovemaking, though of course they can also easily be transported into the bedroom. You can also fool around with plastic wrap, assorted fruits and veggies, ice cubes, and some kitchen gadgets—use your imagination.

Don't take such experimenting too seriously. You're just out to have fun and relieve boredom. By the way, it doesn't matter if you wind up having an orgasm in the kitchen. You can start there and look at whatever you do as foreplay, then retire to the bedroom or to the rug in front of the fireplace. The point of breaking the rules is not to set limits but instead to free yourselves from boring routines.

Some of you are going to worry that if you were to have sex in the kitchen, a room where most people don't have blinds or drapes, that someone might see you. I'm not recommending you become exhibitionists, but there are ways of minimizing this risk, such as making love at night with the lights out or using only candles. Still, in most kitchens this risk will always be present, but the slight possibility you might be discovered could add a certain zest to the sexual episode that might make it a lot more erotic. And, if someone were to knock on the back door, well, you are in your own home so you're not doing anything illegal.

Dining rooms and living rooms, even backyards, offer the same feeling of doing something a little forbidden, with a small risk of being caught that should heighten your level of arousal.

Case study: Carmelina and Tom

Carmelina and Tom both felt their lovemaking had reached a level of excitement concurrent with cutting one's toenails. One day, Carmelina challenged Tom to think of something that would enliven their sex life. Tom, intrigued by the possibilities, immediately agreed to give it some thought. He remembered thirty years before, when they were dating, they both enjoyed necking and petting in the back seat of his old Chevy.

The following Saturday, after dark, Tom took Carmelina's hand and led her to the driveway where their car was parked. He put some oldies in the CD player to set the mood, then ushered his favorite girl into the back seat where they enjoyed some of the best sex they had had in years.

I realize there may be some of my readers who will find such suggestions shocking, or at least feel they would be so uncomfortable having sex anywhere but in their bed that these suggestions are out of the question. Since I am always telling people not to put any pressure on their partners, I'm certainly not going to put pressure on those of you who feel this way. At least not a lot of pressure.

I know some people refuse to try something new because they're afraid if they do it once, if they break their resolve, their partner will hound them to do it again. I accept that there is some truth to this argument. But there's also some truth to the argument that if you don't try something, you can't really know whether or not you'd like it. If you're a parent, then you know how often you tried to get your children to eat certain foods, and many times when they did, they liked it—a lot. So it's quite possible people who refuse to consider making love in the kitchen would get tremendous satisfaction out of actually doing it, but they will never know because they're too afraid to try.

This is another one of those situations where communication and trust are important. First, you have to be willing to talk about such issues with your partner and second, if you agree to try something new because your partner promises, if you hate it, not to bother you with it again, you have to be able to trust that promise.

Of course the other side of the coin is that you have to give it a real shot. If you both go into the kitchen, drop your robes, and then suddenly you grab yours off the floor and wrap up in it saying, "I can't do this!" you didn't really give it a try.

Remember, what I'm suggesting here isn't dangerous. If you're really afraid of getting caught making love in your kitchen, living room, or wherever, set your alarm for three o'clock in the morning, when the only person you're likely to frighten away is a potential burglar, which would be a good outcome!

I'm also sure there are some of you reading this who are saying, "Dr. Ruth, we've already made love in every room in the house, not to mention the front and back yards. How do we spice up our sex

Tip:

One point of doing something different is to lose some of your inhibitions, so it is not surprising if you start out feeling a little inhibited. It's not until you become fully aroused and give in to the moment that you'll be gaining from your new experience.

---

lives?" Such couples have a different problem. Their love life is already quite varied. Their problem has to do with their sexual episodes becoming blasé and my problem is coming up with advice for such people. You see, the bottom line is I'm old fashioned and a square, and they've already done everything I could conceive of and perhaps more. But since it's a legitimate question, here's what I have to say to them.

First of all, when it comes to pleasure and pain, we humans have a way of forgetting the exact sensations caused during these events. If it wasn't like that, after our first orgasm all we'd need to do is remember what happened and never actually have to do it again. So, if such couples experience high levels of arousal and strong orgasms when making love, they have reached their goals. They don't really need to go to another level because they're already getting the most pleasure from sex that they're capable of. What they're looking for is not additional pleasure, but ways to keep sex from becoming boring. And so, to them, my advice is to use their minds to bring as much fantasy into their sex lives as possible.

By fantasy I don't mean kinky sex. I think that's the wrong approach, because sex can only get so kinky and then you hit a dead end. But role-playing types of fantasy are infinite. You can pretend you're the stars of every movie you've seen or book you've read. You can be cave people or pretend to live in the future. Through role-playing you can come up with countless ways to add variety to your love life. The end result, the orgasms that you'll both have while playing out a particular fantasy won't be much different, although, if you find a certain role highly arousing, then one or both of you might have the strongest orgasms you're capable of having. But, as long as your minds are engaged, I can guarantee each of these fantasy enriched sexual episodes will be most gratifying.

Of course, even if you're not among those highly sophisticated couples who've done it all, role-playing can certainly be a rewarding addition to your sexual repertoire. Let's say you go to see a movie that features a couple such as Lancelot and Guinevere. When you get home, put on English accents—don't worry how good you are—and pretend you're back in jolly old England and Lancelot is going to go off to battle the next morning, so you're making love as if it could be for the last time. You'll discover that the experience will be far different than it is when you make love as yourselves.

Will the sex itself be much better? Not necessarily. Some people, women especially, need to concentrate on certain sensations to have an orgasm, and if they're being distracted by the fantasy, they might have some problems. Obviously at that point they should drop the fantasy so they can achieve sexual satisfaction. But remember, the point isn't only to create sexual arousal. You're also trying to keep boredom at bay, so for this purpose playing out a fantasy can be quite rewarding.

And, if you stretch it out, so that now and again during the course of a weekend you put on your roles, this play-acting will become part of your foreplay. You won't just be playing; you'll be sending each other a sexual signal. All this foreplay will have a definite effect when you do begin to make love, that I can assure you.

There can be another advantage to acting out a role. If you're at all shy, you might find it easier to be more sexually aggressive when playing a role. For example, as yourself you might never want to perform fellatio on your partner, but as Guinevere, that might be another story. I'm not saying that will always happen but it can happen. Just think of some of the things you've done in your private sexual fantasies. Most of those remain just that, fantasies, but during role-playing, you might be able to make some of them become real.

There's another advantage to all of this. Let me return to the oral sex example. Some women might be willing to perform oral sex on their partner, but they don't want it to become a regular part of their sex life so they hold back. But, if you perform oral sex only when you're in certain characters, you maintain some control that might make it easier for the two of you to occasionally insert oral sex into your sex play. The same would hold for any other sexual position.

On the one hand, I want to urge you to free yourselves from some of your inhibitions. But on the other hand I don't want you to go too far. Some fantasies and desires are better left unspoken, or, at least, mentioned in a lighthearted manner that won't leave any lasting damage. For example, one sexual position which many people enjoy is anal sex. But others find the thought horrifying. I certainly would not tell you to force yourself to try this if you don't want to. But there's nothing wrong with bringing it up if you're curious about it. You might not want to say, "I want to have anal sex." Instead you might say, "What do you think of anal sex?" If your partner says no in a very strong manner, you can chime in, "I agree," even if you were curious about it. Of course your partner might surprise you by admitting that he or she was also curious, and so you might end up trying it and possibly even liking it and adding it to your regular routine.

Case History: Phil

Phil was a supervisor at a large corporation. The company decided it would be good for morale if employees got to know each other better, and so they brought in facilitators to hold small group sessions. At the session Phil attended, when he saw people were reticent about revealing too much about themselves, he decided he would get the ball rolling by making an admission, which was that he gets turned on by cows. From that moment on, there wasn't one person in the company who when seeing him walking down the hall didn't silently moo to themselves.

Phil's example is kind of extreme. I'm not telling you to stifle every urge, just not to put it on the table too blatantly so your partner will feel like mooing each time he or she looks at you.

Sex toys

Certainly the various articles I mentioned using from the kitchen can be considered sex toys, but when most people use that phrase they're talking about items purchased over the Internet or from a sex shop. There are even women who go into people's homes and sell these products via "parties" like they do Tupperware.

I think the term "sex toy" is a slight misnomer because some of

---

✒ Tip:

What keeps many people away from buying sex toys is the fear of being seen by someone they know as they walk into one of these stores. That you can buy this equipment from a catalogue or online certainly helps, but another suggestion I have is to visit one of these stores in a town where you don't know anybody. This allows you to have a more hands-on experience for your purchase. This strategy also applies to purchasing erotic videos.

Things to Consider Adding to Your Sex Play

- Have phone sex—great when one of you is away on a business trip, or just use your cell phones from room to room in your own home.

- For birthdays and other special occasions, give each other "coupons" to be cashed in for various sexual acts or just relaxing massages.

- Play strip poker, strip Trivial Pursuit, or another game you both enjoy.

- Make your own erotic video (to be erased right afterwards).

- Write down erotic things for one of you to do—either alone or with the other—on slips of paper, then put the slips into a basket. Take turns drawing out one slip and doing what it says on it.

- Exchange clothing.

- Perform a strip tease—men too.

- Blindfold one partner.

- Use feathers, silk, or velvet to caress each other.

- Have sex while one or both of you are fully clothed.

- Engage in mutual masturbation—use hands, shower massages, vibrators, or whatever is handy.

- Have no-hands sex—mouths, feet, legs, everything but hands are allowed.

them are vital to complete sexual satisfaction for some people. There are women who cannot have an orgasm without a vibrator and so to them it's certainly not a toy. And the various lubricants on the market are equally important to women who've gone through menopause.

On the other hand, the term "sex aid" implies you need these items. That's not the case for many people, so this term might make some people shy away from buying or using them. Basically what you call them doesn't matter; if they can liven up your sex life, you shouldn't be afraid of purchasing them.

Sex games

There's a category of board games aimed strictly for couples. Sites that sell erotic material carry such games but you can find quite a selection at drugstore.com, of all places. Among the titles I found were Adultrivia; Allure of Scheherazade: A Magical Eastern Fantasy for Lovers; Bathtub Love: A Bathtub/Hot Tub Game for Lovers; and Strip Chocolate: A Game of Sensual Pleasure. All told, there are several dozen different games, so there's no shortage to choose from. Over the course of time you might try them all, although some are on the expensive side.

Vibrators

I've endorsed one particular vibrator, the Eroscillator, which actually oscillates rather than vibrates, but long before I did that I had been telling women to use them. As I said, for some women, using a vibrator is the only way for them to have an orgasm. They require the strong sensations on or near their clitoris to achieve satisfaction. Other women need a vibrator only to learn how to have an orgasm. Once they realize what an orgasm is, they can then have them in other ways. For women who remain prudish about touching themselves and who don't have a partner, vibrators can help them avoid being sexually frustrated. Other women just like experiencing different types of orgasms and they feel that using a vibrator once in a while is a refreshing change.

Generally, the use of vibrators is safe. The only risk they represent is that some women get hooked on the strong sensations and then can't have an orgasm with a partner. What I recommend is that a woman who needs a vibrator to be orgasmic try to wean herself off of it, even if she doesn't have a partner. She should bring herself close to orgasm with the vibrator and then use her fingers to cause the actual orgasm. After a bit of practice, she may be able to do without the vibrator altogether.

It's not a calamity if a woman cannot have an orgasm any other way than with a vibrator. Couples can integrate the use of a vibrator into their sex life, and after all, the most critical aspect is that she does have an orgasm instead of remaining sexually frustrated. Some women end up needing a vibrator later in life, after having been orgasmic without one, and that's okay too. It's really no different than having to wear glasses in order to see, and no one should be any more ashamed of needing a vibrator than needing glasses.

The tie that binds

Another type of equipment you're likely to find at a sex shop are restraints. Some people who are into sadomasochism use these as part of their sex life. This is not an area of my expertise and so I won't comment on this particular practice. But tying up one's partner once in a while for added sexual excitement is certainly appropriate sex play. The person who is tied up is quite vulnerable and therefore this is a way of building intimacy as well as heightening sexual arousal, at least for some people. If you decide to try it and find it's more frightening than anything else, throw the equipment away. In fact, I recommend you experiment with scarves, men's ties, or other things you already have around the house before investing in equipment you may end up never using.

If the person being restrained asks to be untied, the other partner should do so immediately. No "Ah, honey, just a few more minutes." That attitude is likely to end the sex play abruptly and might even cause one partner to rethink his or her feelings about the entire relationship.

Dildos

Most sex shops have a large selection of dildos. I don't know if they stock these because they sell well or because it's impressive to have all these fake penises on display. Heterosexual couples don't have much of a need for a dildo, unless his equipment isn't working right and she likes the feeling of being filled. Many lesbians, who as a group do use dildos, prefer those which aren't carved to look like a penis, but rather use ones that look like, say, a curved dolphin. That's why I say I guess all the dildos are more for show than anything else.

Penis enhancers

There are rubber sleeves a man can place over his penis that will give him a larger penis. If I've said it once, I've said it a million times, size does not matter. Most women don't care what size penis a man has. It's much more important her partner be a skillful lover. But there are some men who have a very small penis, and there are some women who really need the feeling of their vagina being filled in order to make sex truly satisfying. If one or both of these circumstances are in play in your relationship, then I say go ahead and use one of the penis extenders. Maybe not every time, but at least occasionally.

Now, having said this, if you do decide to add a penis enhancer to your lovemaking paraphernalia, make sure both of you are careful about his ego. None of us have perfect bodies and we could all use a little enhancement in one area or another, but a man's ego is particularly tied to his penis. If you are careful about this subject, you should be able to integrate such a device without wounding his self-respect. The one thing I would beg of you ladies is not to spread this news around. If your partner found out you were telling your girlfriends about it, he would be awfully embarrassed.

Lingerie

In this day and age where young women wear next to nothing on the beach and a thong instead of complete underwear, I don't suppose many young women use the type of lacy lingerie that was once a de rigueur gift for a woman off on her honeymoon. But older women, whose bodies have some imperfections due to aging may find sexy lingerie is a worthwhile investment. Men tend to love lingerie because it feels like they are seeing something they're not supposed to be seeing or that the woman is being "naughty."

📌 Tip:

Ladies, if you think lingerie is silly but your partner doesn't, don't be quick to look down your nose at a gift from him of something sheer and lacy. It definitely shows he's still interested in your body and for this you should be grateful, not annoyed.

While I'm on the subject of sexy lingerie, which may not be something you want to wear regularly, I want to say a few words about what you do normally wear to bed. Whatever your typical outfit is, from nothing to flannel pajamas, do understand your clothing choice makes a statement. If you're always covered head to toe, you appear unavailable. If this is the message you always want to send, this is a problem which needs to be addressed. But, if you're covering yourself up without giving a thought to the effect it has on your spouse, I want to raise your level of awareness about the message you are sending.

Obviously, if it's a freezing night, cover up, but at other times, don't be afraid of wearing clothing that, if not actually revealing, can easily be removed or moved aside. And when you're not in bed, just lounging around, try not to wear the same old grungy clothes all the time. I know we all have favorite items that in and of themselves give comfort because they somehow convey relaxation, but sometimes these items can get a bit ratty and that's not sexy. It's great to be comfortable, but accept the fact that you can be comfortable and still dress somewhat attractively. This advice applies to men too.

Sex swings

I often joke about making love while swinging from a chandelier, but let's face it, that's a ridiculous idea and very dangerous, unless it's on a movie set. But you can actually buy harnesses which can be attached to the ceiling or to a frame made for this purpose that stands on the ground.

Do I recommend you go out and purchase these devices? If you're of a certain age, using one might be a bit awkward and difficult or even risky—and they're costly and a bit complicated to use. On the other hand, people spend thousands of dollars to go on second hon-

Some people with bad backs actually find such a swing makes sex more comfortable.

---

eymoons and love cruises just to spark up their sex life, so if you think having one of these gizmos would add enough spice to amortize the cost, go right ahead.

These swings allow you to try all sorts of positions that would otherwise be impossible, so, when it comes to getting rid of boredom in the bedroom, they'll certainly help. The best thing about having sex while the woman is hanging in midair and the man is standing is that he can reach her clitoris while they're having intercourse, thus making it more likely she'll have an orgasm while his penis is inside of her. For some couples this is very important, and, if one of these swings can fulfill this need, buying one may be quite a reasonable decision.

There's one category of items which can be purchased in a sex shop that I've skipped over, and that's erotica. Because there are several aspects to erotica, some of which are negative, I'm going to devote an entire chapter to it, in fact, the next one. So please read on for my views on this subject.

ℬ
Erotica

You may be saying to yourselves right about now, "Dr. Ruth is giving us a whole chapter on erotica so she must have been busy lately looking at some pretty wild videos and Web sites to recommend." Sorry to disappoint you, but I'm going to let you do your own research when it comes to choosing such material. While I am in favor of people using erotica, there is far too much of it that is not done very well and I leave it to others to sift through the good, the bad, and the downright ugly.

So, while I didn't do extensive research before writing this chapter, it's not that I haven't seen a lot of erotica, from a variety of films to ancient Chinese drawings, most recently at an exhibit at New York's Museum of Sex.

At this point I want to say something about the terminology. When referring to photos and films that depict sexual activity, many people use the word "porn," short for pornography. To them, anything that might arouse the viewer is pornographic. But since I believe the more people are aroused the better, I don't want to attach a word that has negative connotations to material that arouses people. To me, a film depicting two people having sex isn't pornographic but is merely erotic. Now if a film shows minors having sex with adults or bestiality or people who are being forced to have sex or endure pain, that, to me, is pornography. But while there is material that fits my definition of porn out there, the vast majority of what people call porn is merely erotica.

For the most part I approve of people using erotica to spice up their sex life, be it singles who use it for masturbation or couples to get themselves aroused before having sex. But I also recognize there can be a downside to using erotica, and I will cover both the positive and negative aspects in this chapter. In fact, I was prompted to devote an entire chapter to this subject because of some recent complications related to erotica that have been brought to my attention.

Let me start with the pros. At the risk of stating the obvious, erotic videos can be arousing. If your love life needs a bit of a spark,

Films to Watch For

There were a couple of short films that I used to show in my college classes. One featured a close-up of someone peeling an orange, that, believe it or not, was very erotic. Another was an old film of two people having sex that was speeded up, making it funny rather than sexy. I've also recommended to older couples a film called "A Ripple In Time" that features older adults having sex. Given how few role models there are for older adults when it comes to sex, having some of my patients see other older people enjoying sex helped them to overcome some of their reticence. I also think seeing this film would be a good lesson for younger audiences as it might help to remove some of the prejudice of ageism. It may still be available somewhere, though it would take some searching to find it as it was made in 1974.

watching a film that shows couples engaging in all sorts of sexual situations could be just the thing to put you in the proper mood.

Now I readily admit that there are people who can't stand these films or the many magazines that show naked bodies. Many women, in particular, don't like being compared to the exaggerated female forms that populate such material, and, of course, some men don't like to have their equipment compared to the studs that are hired for such films either. In addition, there are women who can't stomach the idea of making love to their partner after he's been aroused looking at someone else's breasts...or whatever. And many others object to this type of material for religious reasons.

I absolutely respect these points of view, and no one should be forced to watch something that doesn't appeal to them. But, if you don't share in these negative feelings, then I see nothing wrong in watching an erotic movie to increase your level of arousal. Of course, even if both partners agree on watching erotica, that doesn't mean that they'll be any closer to agreeing on which film to watch than they are when they go to Blockbuster and he wants an action film and she wants a chick flick. And since these films aren't reviewed in your local paper, choosing one can be hit or miss. But since none of us expect to find academy award material in these films, I would urge you not to be too picky.

📌 Tip:

There is a genre of erotic films made by women to appeal to women. Candida Royale is one producer of such films. These films have much more of a plot than the standard fare, and while they're certainly very explicit, many women find them more appealing to watch than the films that are made mostly to please a male audience. Most men don't mind watching this genre of film either, especially if it encourages their partner to allow such films to be brought into their home to share in the first place.

One type of explicit video that's on the market are the ones that are instructional in nature. You're supposed to purchase these so you and your partner can learn some new and improved sex techniques. I'm not sure how much of an educational value they have though, since the sex scenes are interrupted from time to time by "experts" doing a lot of talking. But, if in your mind you find it more acceptable to watch people having sex in the context of a lesson, and if these videos also increase both partners' level of arousal, by all means use them to enhance your sex life. After all, you may even learn a thing or two.

Getting erotic videos

As you may know, the large chains, like Blockbuster, don't carry any erotic films. Smaller stores do, but some people are afraid they'll run into a neighbor and wind up being embarrassed. One simple solution is not to go to your neighborhood video store. Instead drive a few miles away where the odds are a lot less that anyone there will know you.

You can also purchase or rent videocassettes and DVDs on the Internet. See the "Resources" section at the back of the book for some of these Web sites. If you have a high-speed connection, you also may be able to download a video directly into your home computer. And many cable and satellite providers feature erotic films you can pay to view.

Have we gone too far?

Sexual images have been around for thousands of years. The very earliest sculptures we've found are of fertility goddesses with exaggerated breasts and buttocks. But in the recent past, the capacity to view erotic art has developed by leaps and bounds. We went from paintings to still photographs to grainy black and white films. We added magazines with color photos on nearly every newsstand, produced color movies that became instant classics and crossed over into wide audiences made up of both sexes. Then the technology came along that allowed these movies to be seen in the privacy of people's bedrooms. And, most recently, homes have been given access to the almost limitless amount of material, both stills and video, available on the Internet.

It's the latter medium that concerns me at the moment because it seems to have caused some major changes in how these materials are being used.

Case History: Laura and Tom

It was the second marriage for both Laura and Tom and, for the first four years, they enjoyed an exciting and rewarding sex life. Then they got broadband so downloading images and videos became much easier on their computer. At first Laura didn't realize the cause, but she noticed Tom was becoming less and less interested in having sex with her. One night she woke up to find his side of the bed empty. She tiptoed out of the room and discovered him in the den masturbating while looking at an erotic video he had downloaded. Only a few hours before, he had turned her down when she'd tried to initiate having sex. Immediately Laura realized this wasn't an isolated incident; she was looking at the cause of their dried-up sex life. She, of course, exploded in tears, ran back to the bedroom, slamming and locking the door.

There have always been people, mostly men, who have been

hooked on erotica to the extent that they prefer to masturbate than have sex with a real person. But, while I don't have scientific data to back me up, I believe the segment of the male population who practiced this pattern of behavior used to be smaller. Nor have I seen a scientific study on the effects this new easy access to erotica has had on the population. But I have enough anecdotal evidence to say that in some households this material has caused quite a problem, and I'm afraid that it is more widespread than is publicly acknowledged.

The basis for my concern comes from the questions people ask me, either in letters or on the Web. I'm hearing from far too many women who say their husbands aren't having sex with them any more, preferring to masturbate after downloading erotic images. Apparently there is something about searching the Web for sexual images that goes beyond even the ease of popping a video into the VCR that has hooked these men.

There can be other factors explaining men's preferring to masturbate rather than to have sex with their partner. One is the busy lives we all lead. Good sex takes time and energy, and some men feel the trade isn't worth it. For men who are just being lazy, the erotica they find on the Web isn't the source of the problem but rather is just the means to getting sexual satisfaction without putting out too much effort. Yet many of these men spend hours surfing the Web, so for them, that pretty much removes the issue of this type of sex being a time-saver.

I think the fact women have become more demanding in terms of sex is also a factor. Women usually take longer to have an orgasm than men. There was a time, not too long ago, when many women never had orgasms, and so men could put as much or as little energy into having sex as they wanted. While taking your time when making love is certainly preferable to always engaging in quickies, some men don't always want to expend the energy needed to please their partners. There are men who, when faced with a woman who expects to have an orgasm, find masturbation an easy way out, especially when combined with the ease of access to erotica.

But, while these things might lead men to masturbate once in a while instead of having sex, the women who are asking me questions are finding their partners never want to have sex. In such cases, there are serious repercussions with regard to the relationship. I'm sure these men know what they are doing isn't right, but they can't seem to stop themselves.

Let me offer one theory why I believe the Internet in particular has complicated this behavior. As we've all noticed, once remote control devices came into existence, and especially after they were combined with hundreds of available channels on cable, men and women began to watch TV differently. Many men seem to use the remote to turn watching TV into a form of hunting. Their curiosity about what might be on another channel keeps them from remaining interested in any one channel. I'm guessing the same sort of response might be going on with regard to erotica on the Web.

There are literally millions of images of naked women on the Web, many of which can be seen for free. Others require some sort of paid subscription, although the subscriptions aren't terribly expensive. I've read that sex-related sites get more hits than any other type of material on the Web. As long as the demand is there, there will be material produced to lure viewers. With all this erotic material available on every home computer, it seems some men cannot keep themselves from hunting through it. They may not know exactly what they're looking for, but the sheer volume and variety has an irresistible pull on them, similar to the way they hunt around the TV dial. Of course after spending time looking at all these images they become aroused. They're often ashamed to admit what they've been doing to their spouse, so to relieve the sexual stimulation they are feeling, they masturbate. That, in turn, removes their desire for sex, so they stop having sex with their partner.

Of course this is a very simplified explanation and probably one of many. (For instance, when the man really doesn't want to have sex with his wife, the Web offers him an alternative. In this scenario, access to Web-based erotica isn't the underlying problem.) What I'm saying is, perhaps for a group of men, maybe even a large group, it's not just the sexual lure that is working here. It's not that these males are looking to avoid having sex with their partners, it's just that they can't stop themselves from hunting around to see what images are available on the Web. The ease with which this material is available has made it too tempting for them to resist. Once there, they get excited and masturbate. And while there's nothing wrong with masturbation per se, when someone masturbates so much that they don't want to have sex with their partner, this becomes a big problem.

While this effect is happening across all age groups, it may be having an even more serious effect among older men. That's because the desire for sex in older men is less strong than in younger men. Therefore, such erotic Web surfing, even if the men only do it once a week, can have an even more serious impact on their sex life with their partners. If a couple's sex life has dwindled down to once a week and instead he is masturbating once a week while surfing the Web, this leaves her entirely out in the cold.

There's an additional problem with older men that has to be kept in mind. If an older man has been having problems with his erections, he may find that the stimulus of erotica, combined with the particular knowledge he has of how to please himself with his hand, may make masturbation in front of the computer the only possible way for him to enjoy sex—or at least he might think so.

Case History: John and Lannie

Lannie had desperately wanted to go for a weekend to a resort with some friends of theirs, but when John's boss asked him to work that weekend, he had forgotten about it and agreed. Once he'd committed, he couldn't change his mind so they weren't able to go away. When Lannie found this out, the day before they were set to leave, she became furious. Her eruption made John equally angry, and rather than meekly sleep in the den, he went online and spent several hours surfing every sex site he could find.

Lannie's temper remained at the boiling point the next day. She refused to speak to him or let him back in the bedroom, so he repeated the exercise that night. The next day she had cooled down, but John had found his surfing episodes so enjoyable he started staying up late nights to surf the Web, even after he was once again sleeping in the bedroom. Their sex life took a serious turn for the worse. Lannie blamed it on her overreaction to that one weekend, never suspecting John had found this new outlet for his sexual needs.

As I said, the reasons a couple stop having sex can be complex. It's rarely just one factor. If two people love each other very much and have had a good sex life, I doubt the lure of the Web is going to pull them apart permanently. Every relationship has some cracks in it, which is why many are vulnerable to unexpected pressures. But pressures have always been there. I believe something else is going on here, and since so many women are reporting that their husbands are looking at erotica on the Internet, I can't help but assume that it is the medium itself, not just the erotica, which has always been around, that is adding to the problem.

To some degree this resembles what happens to addicted gamblers when betting becomes more available. When giving in to the urge to gamble meant a cross-country trip to Las Vegas, many Americans who might have had a problem with gambling didn't because the opportunities for gambling weren't as available. (Of course those who were bitten with this bug could get around it via illegal bookies, etc.) But, when Indian casinos and slot machines started to appear all over the place, many more people began having a hard time keeping themselves from gambling away their life savings.

If I'm right, if this is a type of addiction, then couples have to work together to overcome it. The first step is for the man to admit he has a problem, but, as you can imagine, getting to this first step is often difficult. Since these men know what they are doing is wrong and are possibly embarrassed about it, they're not going to want to admit to it. If they are truly addicted, they also aren't going to want to put this habit at risk.

Most of the women who write in say their husbands deny they are doing it. Yet it is easy enough to prove if the men don't erase the history of where they've been surfing that remains on the computer, or if the man is caught doing it red-handed, so to speak, night after night.

If you have ascertained that your partner is engaging in this behavior to the detriment of your sex life together, you do need to deal with it. But it is easy to fall into the trap of dealing with it inappropriately.

Let me put one thing on the table: I'm against issuing threats, no matter how tempting a reaction that might be. When faced with this type of situation, it's a natural reaction for the woman to say, "Either you stop this behavior or I'm leaving you." This may be the natural reaction, but that doesn't make it the one that's going to be the most useful. That's because, if someone is addicted to a habit, such an approach rarely works. It's possible, if the couple were to actually separate, an addicted man might see the light and change, but taking things to that level is often counterproductive and certainly endangers the relationship.

And, while it's tempting to get angry and start a fight over such matters, you're better off resisting this temptation. As I said, the first step is to get him to admit that this is a problem. Having a calm conversation about it is the place to start. If your partner continues to deny his behavior, what I advise is for you to suggest putting a filter on your home computer that stops erotica from being viewed or downloaded. These filters are often available on the Web free or for little cost on the Web. If your partner accepts this, then maybe you were wrong and the addiction wasn't real. Or maybe he is ashamed of his behavior, wants help, and will actually be relieved that you are offering this solution. In any case, once the filter is installed, the temptation will be removed, and, if your sex life together picks up, the problem is solved.

But what if your partner refuses to allow this? Of course this is likely an admission of guilt. But it is also a cry for help. Most addicts, no matter what they are addicted to, realize they have a problem, but they don't know how to kick their habit. And in many cases, their life-partners don't have the expertise or are too close to the situation to help them. The solution, if this is the case, is to get professional help.

If you are faced with such a situation, my advice is to see a sex therapist or a marital counselor. Your partner, the addicted person, may not be willing to go along at first. Don't let that stop you. Together with the help of your therapist, you may be able to convince your partner to attend a session or two. It is hopeful, at that point, that your partner will be able to make enough progress to get the problem under control.

What if there is no progress, if your partner refuses to address the issue? What if you've spent thirty, forty, or fifty years together, and now because of his addiction to erotica your sex life is over? Is this enough of a reason to leave him? That is a very, very difficult question. Getting to the right answer for you is not going to be simple. Again, seeing a professional counselor will be of help. An important aspect of this is being able to come to terms with your decision, especially if it's to stay married even if he won't change. How are you going to deal with a sexless marriage? If your decision is to stay in a sexless marriage, you will need to find a way of coping with your feelings. If you're going to always be angry, your health and happiness will suffer.

Of course, if you are one of the women we discussed earlier who don't wish to continue having sexual relations with their spouse, his addiction to Web-based erotica might be exactly what you're looking for. This, of course, is a shame, since, in my opinion, adults who do not have an enjoyable sex life, regardless of age, are missing out on one of the most wonderful things about being a human being.

Cyber chatting

While looking at erotic images tends to be a pastime mostly pursued by men, there's another type of sexual attraction offered by the Internet that can be attractive to either sex. This is the lure of the chat room. Married people go on line, using some pseudonym, and pretend they're single, as well as beautiful, young, and sexy. It starts out as a game, but sometimes they meet someone with whom a connection forms. That connection certainly takes away from the emotional ties this person has with his or her spouse. If the chatterers start having cybersex, masturbating separately while chatting sexually, this drives an even bigger wedge between husband and wife. And, if they make the transition from cyber space to real life, that's called "having an affair," and the relationship is definitely in jeopardy.

When is chatting cheating? It's a question I get asked quite often, and I suppose the answer depends on the degree and content. Obviously if two people share a hobby, find each other on a chat line, and spend time chatting, that's not much different from an ordinary friendship. But as soon as one person hides the fact that he or she is married or the subject of the discussion becomes sexual, dangerous territory has been entered. There may be no cheating going on yet, but the door is wide open.

Of course some people who admit to being married decide their chat mate offers them more than their real life spouse. But when that happens, my guess is that the marriage wasn't in very good shape to begin with, though I suppose the flirting that goes on does put even sound marriages on dangerous grounds.

So, while sexual chatting may not strictly constitute cheating, it definitely may lead to it and that's a risk to which you shouldn't subject your marriage.

Other types of erotica

As I mentioned earlier, I used to show a film that was a close-up of someone peeling an orange in the classes I taught and used it for years in my college lectures as well. It may sound hard to believe, but watching this film is definitely arousing, even though there isn't a nude body anywhere. For something to be erotic doesn't mean it has to show two people engaging in sex acts or even nudity. I've written several books that feature material that is definitely erotic but most of which is quite short of what anyone would consider pornographic. The visual elements in these books are mostly artworks that hang in museums, and, while some of these reproductions do contain nudes, many don't. And yet the images are all very erotic.

I'm not bringing this up to get you to go out and buy another one of my books (though, if you happen to purchase either *The Art of*

Arousal or *The Lovers Companion: Art and Poetry of Desire* I wouldn't object) but to offer you another suggestion, especially if one of you doesn't care for the more explicit erotica. Because these types of work are considered fine art, they become more acceptable. And yet because they do have erotic content, looking at such images together can lift one's spirits, so to speak. So, if looking at videos is too much for one or both of you, try looking at books that contain art works that are less graphic than what you'll find in a triple-X movie. These images can be very arousing, particularly if you concentrate on everything that is going on in each scene.

There is also a genre of erotica that features no images at all. The written word can certainly be used to titillate, and perhaps the partner who doesn't want to share in the experience of looking at images might find reading this type of erotica more to his or her liking. There are classic books, like my favorite, *Lady Chatterley's Lover*, and many newer works written mainly to arouse. A number of these are published expressly for women. There are also Web sites that feature erotic writing. Some even let you post your own erotic stories. (Writing one together might be excellent foreplay.) Such written material may be used in addition to the visual forms of erotica or may provide an acceptable compromise for those who are uncomfortable with these more graphic types. If one of you is ill at ease with films and such, I suggest you at least try some of these erotic stories.

Making your own erotica

Another option is to make your own erotica using a digital or video camera. Now I have to give you one important caveat when bringing up this possibility: You have to be very careful that no one else ever stumbles on such images. Ironically, one day as I was working on this chapter, a woman posted on one of my message boards that the twenty-three-year-old son of her lover had found naughty pictures of her and his father on the father's computer. If you take such pictures, assume they will be found unless you are extremely careful about where you keep them. It is often great fun to make your own erotica, just be ultra careful how and where you store them.

I suggest using a digital camera. Not only is the issue of a lab technician seeing the images (and making his own copies?) when developing the film removed, but the images can easily be erased right after your play session.

As with viewing erotica, sometimes one partner will refuse to pose for such pictures. This may be especially true if this person has issues with body image. Now, as I've said over and over again in this book, I'm against pressuring people to do anything they don't want to, but perhaps, in this case, a little pressure would be all right. By a little pressure, I mean asking nicely a second or third time, highlighting the fact that the images can be instantly deleted. I say this light pressure might be all right because it's possible that people with a body image problem would see themselves differently in a photograph. By seeing themselves as their partner sees them, these people might be able to realize that their body is sexy.

Of course if someone objects on religious or moral grounds, no such pressure should be applied. But if their negative reaction is mostly about body image, then it might be useful to do some prodding.

Final word

We humans find ways of abusing almost everything. There's a long list of -aholics, everything from chocolate to shopping, alcohol to drugs. Sex can obviously be abused too, and erotica can be a part of this abuse. But just as most people know how to moderate their use of alcohol, the majority of people who turn to erotica from time to time for sexual stimulation don't go overboard. For most people, using erotica to spice up their sex life is quite all right. For those who can't control themselves, let me repeat what I've said over and over throughout this book, if you run into trouble over a sexual issue, get professional help.

9

The Pitfalls of Retirement

Scattered here and there in this book I've mentioned some of the pitfalls that later life can place in front of a couple, including such issues as empty nest syndrome and various health problems that can arise. I realize many people look forward to retirement with great expectations but, when it comes to reality, sometimes retirement can bring more problems than pleasures.

Often one of the main complications of retirement is insufficient finances, but, since I'm not an expert in finances, that's an area where I'm only going to scratch the surface , although I want to mention some of the emotional bumps in the road money problems can bring. Emotional bumps, as we've seen, can negatively affect your sex life.

It may surprise you that if one or both partners are forced to work past the retirement age, there can actually be some benefits to the relationship. However, because your health may begin to suffer as you get older, to plan on continuing to work may be problematic. That's why it's certainly better to have enough resources so that when you reach your upper sixties, you can retire if you want to or have to.

But as I said, I'm not a financial expert so my main focus in this chapter will be to help you to deal with the psychological, emotional, and sexual issues that may arise, either directly or indirectly due to retirement. In order to make certain none of these becomes serious, you have to face them and deal with them.

For example, if you're already retired and it seems as if you're getting more and more irritated at each other, don't blame it on getting older or being retired. Yes, some older people seem to get more and more cranky as they age, but if you blame any bitterness you feel toward a partner on old age, you're doomed to remain bitter forever. On the other hand, if you say this is a problem like any other and there's a solution, then you can take some positive measures to improve your circumstances.

A sudden change

While getting older is a gradual process, retirement is often a sudden and enormous change. You can't rely solely on the fact you've been together for a long time to get you through this. You are going to have to adapt to this change, and in order for the adaptations to be mostly positive ones, you have to put in the time and energy needed to mold them correctly. Left to chance, your relationship could suffer from the transition to the retirement years, and it would be a great pity for the final decades of your life not to be at their optimum.

Case Study: Tim and Laura

Tim's brother and sister had both moved to California when they were in their thirties. Each time Tim and his wife, Laura, visited his siblings, they would talk about how, when they retired, they should move from Boston and settle nearby. When Tim was sixty-three, he got a large bonus, and, on a trip out to California for the holidays, he made an appointment with a real estate agent to look at some condominiums. He hadn't told Laura, who became very upset when she found out. While she liked visiting out west, she had no real desire to move to California, especially since most of her relatives lived in and around Boston. She refused to go looking at places, no matter how much Tim begged, and their time spent out west was far from enjoyable.

Great expectations

One area that can cause problems occurs when two partners have different expectations for their retirement years and don't talk about them ahead of time. If he's thinking that they're going to move to some warmer climate where he can play golf every day while she's imagining they will stay put so she can spend as much time as she likes with their grandchildren, you can see they have a problem to resolve. Perhaps the solution will be as easy as becoming "snowbirds," spending a few months of the year in a southern state, or perhaps one of them will willingly agree to modify, to one degree or another, his or her vision of what retired life will be like.

When two people spend many years together, it's quite easy to assume you're on the same wavelength, when in reality you're at opposite poles. That's why it's vital to put aside time to talk about your retirement plans. Retirement is not like a vacation. If, on a vacation, you end up going someplace or doing something one partner doesn't particularly like, a couple of weeks is not that large a chunk of time, and you can probably make it up to the displeased partner with the next vacation. But your retirement years could end up being a large percentage of your life. If one of you is miserable for all those years, that's a very serious matter—partially because miserable people and their spouses rarely have the wonderful sex lives all of us deserve.

Of course, even if you do talk about where and how you are going to spend your retirement, it's quite possible you'll not be able to reach an agreement that completely satisfies both parties. And, because of finances, your options may be more limited than you assumed. You may think you'll be the ones to decide whether or not you move or how you'll spend your time, but that may not necessarily be the case. Circumstances could determine the outcome. Would an outcome vastly different from the one a partner had hoped for be enough to break up the relationship? Certainly it depends on the relationship, but it also depends on how you've dealt with this problem over a longer period of time.

There are many people who get married thinking that once they've signed on the dotted line they're going to get the other person to change. Most of the time that doesn't happen, and so one or both parties end up disappointed. The same phenomenon occurs with regard to retirement. He's always talking about how great it's going to be when they retire to Florida and he can buy a skiff and fish every day. She keeps silent, knowing that when the time comes she's going to put her foot down and refuse any such move. And that's when the fireworks are going to begin.

If the first time she hears him dreaming aloud about his retirement days in Florida she tells him her ideas are quite different, and, over time, he learns to accept that they aren't on the same page on this matter, it won't be such a problem when they reach their retirement years. They may have a few fights over it during the intervening period, fights she might have avoided by keeping silent on the issue, but these disagreements shouldn't shake the relationship irreparably. But if she brings a dream he's had for a decade or more crashing down just as he is about to realize it, especially if he's been bragging about it to all and sundry to the point his ego is heavily invested in it, irreparable harm could come to their relationship. They might stay together but he might truly resent her forever. Their entire retirement years might be quite chilly ones, and not because they remained up north but because they didn't do a good job of communicating.

Case History: Norma and Chuck

Chuck was a trial lawyer. There was nothing he loved better than sinking his teeth into a case and then getting up in court and winning over a jury. He was the happiest when he had to spend a string of sleepless nights preparing for a trial. He didn't really have any hobbies, and the more hours he worked, the better he felt.

His wife, Norma, taught kindergarten. She loved the little ones in her care, but while their energy never gave out, as she grew older hers was rapidly disappearing. When she was offered the opportunity to retire at age sixty, she grabbed it. She knew she'd have to wait a bit for Chuck to retire, but she dreamed of the days they could sail around the Caribbean for weeks at a time. The only problem was, ten years later, Chuck was still going strong, with no signs that he might ever retire, and Norma was getting sick and tired of waiting.

Differing time tables

There's another broad area that can produce strong disagreements and that's the decision of when to retire. Let's say she loves her job and doesn't want to ever retire, while he has grown to dislike his and can't wait until he reaches sixty-five. Or she's eight years younger than he is and her career is really booming, while his is starting to rapidly fade.

It's impossible to predict the future. Some people don't like to think about their retirement because it worries them. They may feel, if they start to think about the good times they'll have, they'll jinx themselves. Or they may feel it's so far away, why get all worked up over it now? But, as the examples I've shown you illustrate, by remaining silent, you're laying a trap for yourselves. If one of you develops some very high expectations, the disappointment felt by that partner when his or her dream doesn't come true will be hard to bear. So, while you don't have to plan out every detail of what your retirement may be, do talk about the broad strokes and try to settle some basic issues. If you know ahead of time that you're not going to be able to get your way, you can begin to figure out what compromises you can live with. For example, if you had imagined retiring at sixty-five and you discover your partner has no intention of stopping work when you hit that magic number, then, even if you leave your current job, you should be looking at how you're going to fill the hours. Perhaps you'll start a new career or do volunteer work or go back to school. Or maybe your decision will be to stick it out longer so you're not stuck at home by yourself. You could plan to put away the additional income from those extra years at the job to fund whatever it is you'd like to do when you both retire. Whatever your situation, the more planning you do, the better.

Talking to a wall

Now sometimes, when you communicate your feelings to your spouse and he or she answers with "We'll cross that bridge when we get to it" or some other noncommittal response, you may assume the air has been cleared when it hasn't been at all.

If your partner seems to be agreeing to your plans too easily or, if he or she has a history of stalling for time, you just have to be firmer, maybe even putting your message and what you think the two of you have agreed to in writing.

If you're pretty sure he dreams of buying twenty acres in a distant state and becoming a gentleman farmer and, then, when you say you want to stay in an urban area, he immediately agrees, be suspicious. Don't take the easy way out and say to yourself, "Great, he agreed to what I want." Better to hash this all out ahead of time than at the last minute. If you're ten years away from retirement, you can arrive at a compromise. But if you're six months away, it may not be possible.

Arriving at a compromise

How do you reach such compromises? Let's take this particular issue again, where to live after you're retired. Part of that decision will be based on each of your likes and dislikes. But there will also be very practical matters like costs and where your family lives. I would recommend that together you examine this topic from every angle. Figure out what the cost differences would be. For example, if you moved south, your heating bills would go down, but since you'd want to see your grandchildren, your transportation costs would go up. Sit down and work out the details. The most important part of this exercise is that, in the end, you'll each have a better understanding of your partner's desires.

Let's say he wants to move south, but he also loves his grandchildren. Once he sees that he'd miss being a part of his grandchildren's lives as they grow up, he might be willing give up his dream of playing golf in winter. On the other hand, maybe you really hate the cold of winter and wouldn't mind being a snowbird for a quarter of the year, especially if the grandchildren could come down and visit you. So don't stick your heads in the sand. Instead, face these issues head on, open up a continuing dialogue (not a continuing battle— there's a difference) and I really do believe that you'll come to a solution that will make you both happy.

Other challenges

Now I want to warn you of some of the other potholes you might encounter.

Setting a budget: Adjusting to a new level of income needs to be thought out ahead of time. If one partner is a big spender, curbing those habits may not be easy. I deal with this issue in greater depth later in this chapter.

Household chores: When you're both retired and have the same amount of free time, this is an area that needs to be negotiated. For example, the fact that he likes to cook but makes a big mess and doesn't clean up, might not have been a problem when he rarely did it. But if he wants to cook regularly, the clean-up duties have to be carefully negotiated.

Morning doves vs. night owls: When work constrained the two of you, your hours may have been in some sort of synch. But without a particular need to get up, that might change and require some adjustments. If he likes to sleep in and you relish getting up to watch the 6 A.M. news and the sound of the TV wakes him up, you both have a problem.

As I've been saying throughout this book, calm, non-accusatory communication about these problems is the way to resolve them.

Getting on each other's nerves

Of course talking about all these issues and reaching some agreements doesn't mean your plans are going to turn out exactly the way you dreamed. As I touched upon in an earlier chapter, if you've spent most of your married life apart because one or both of you were off at work each weekday, it's quite possible spending every waking hour together will be more than you can bear. It's possible you got on each other's nerves somewhat before you retired, but it wasn't critical because you spent so little time together. But change that equation significantly, and you're going to come up with a different picture altogether.

So, if you find yourselves in this situation, what do you do?

Again, the best solution is to find things to do together that you both enjoy, so you're not just sitting in the same room glaring at each other, or even worse, staying in separate rooms avoiding each other. One simple thing you could do would be to see what continuing education courses are available at nearby colleges and sign up for some classes. Maybe you'll wind up taking the same course, or maybe you'll each choose something different, but at least you'll be sharing the overall experience. And either way, being out of the house and meeting new people and reading homework assignments will all give you new things to talk about, so when you are together, you're less likely to be bored with each other's company.

Of course there are dozens of other things you could do besides taking courses, including getting interested in a new sport, adopting a hobby, or just going for long walks together. There's also the entire area of volunteer activities. If you've got your health, there are plenty of places to volunteer, ranging from houses of worship to schools, senior facilities, and hospitals. Again, the object is to get out of the house and get some stimulation that you can use later on to give a positive boost to your relationship.

Setting up a schedule

If you follow this advice and lead an active life-style, I would advise you to set up a written schedule. If one of you plays bridge, for example, let the other partner know exactly when you'll be gone so he or she can make his or her own plans. It's often quite aggravating to find out at the last minute you have a free afternoon and nothing to fill it with. And, if you've become a bit more forgetful than before, having a schedule posted on the refrigerator will be useful to avoid these types of conflicts as well as to remind yourself what you have planned.

Now pay attention, this is important: On this schedule, make sure you pencil in some spots for love making. If your energy level tends to become somewhat depleted, it's important to know ahead of time that you're going to have to build up your reserves in anticipation of these sessions. I'm not saying not to make love spontaneously; of course you should do that too whenever possible. But to insure your sex life stays afloat, scheduling time for sex is a good safety net. This is especially true if he needs to take a pill in order to achieve an erection. This requirement will make the window of opportunity smaller, making scheduling even more appropriate.

Don't get mad, get moving

Another key to avoiding major conflicts is exercise. When you get mad, even if you're not showing it yet, your level of adrenaline goes up. When that happens, the fight or flight reflex kicks in. In other words, you're ready for some action. If you end up just sitting there, all that pent-up energy will find a way out, often verbally. So by doing something physical, just about anything, you can weaken the coming storm. It could be as simple as taking a walk. Or picking up a five-pound weight and doing some arm exercises (but don't throw it at anyone). Or vacuuming the living room. Anything to use up that negative energy doing something positive.

At that point, should you do something physical together? Some couples find a good fight stimulates them sexually. If that's been the case between the two of you most of your lives, go right ahead. But most people don't follow that pattern, so maybe when you're angry it would be better to separate a bit so you can cool down. Of course there's nothing stopping you from falling into each other's arms after the storm has passed.

And, if you've spent a lifetime of laughing together at this and that, don't forget to use humor to diffuse a situation. It doesn't have to be a witty remark, but can be plain old slapstick. Stick your head under the kitchen faucet. Drop an ice cube down his shirt. Pull down your pants and moon each other. There are plenty of ways to vent your anger while still being funny.

Living longer

I want to say something serious at this point. When people developed the concept of marriage, very few people lived to the ages that we Westerners commonly reach today. Let's face it, spending thirty, forty, fifty years or more with the same person is going to pose some challenges. Yes, you're familiar with each other's habits, which brings a certain level of comfort, and yes, you love each other, but it's not so hard to also drive each other crazy after so many years. There have been good times and there have been bad times, but most of all there's been a lot of time.

It's okay to get a little upset with your partner because there's also so much glue to hold you together. I'm not saying you should fight, but if you do, it's not the end of the world, nor is it unexpected. If the fighting becomes the norm, that's another story. Maybe at that point you need some professional intervention. But you have to learn to expect the occasional spat. And the best way of healing any wounds that open up because of these set-tos, after you've calmed down, is to hold each other for a long, long time.

The empty nest fills up

There's another situation that's befalling some retirees—their children who left the nest long ago come back as adults. This return home may be a result of divorce or job downsizing. Divorce may mean only one person joins you, but when jobs are lost, often the returning child brings his or her spouse. In either case, your grandchildren may also move in. Suddenly your retirement plans get turned topsy-turvy, and instead of being just the two of you, there's three, four, or five of you.

First of all, look at this on the bright side. It may mess up your sex life as your turns to dust, but having your children and grandchildren around should be a good thing—assuming you all get along. Again, you have to have open communication between you and your partner, but you also have to have it as a group. Let each adult have their say, because, after all, your grown children and their spouses are full-fledged adults. Among the things to discuss is setting a goal that defines the length of time until they get themselves resettled. Try to come up with compromises you can all live with.

And by the way, don't forget your children also have sex lives of their own now, so while they may be impinging on yours, you're also impinging on theirs. While you don't have to openly say why, try to give each other some space. If you decide to go to the movies, make sure your children know ahead of time so they can plan on using any private moments fully.

Sandwich generation

In this new millennium, just because you're of retirement age doesn't necessarily mean your parents have passed away. There are many people living today who are in the eighties, nineties, and beyond, and one or both of your parents could fall into this category. (Actually you have four opportunities for this to happen, and with blended parents, it might even be higher than that.) This can definitely be a burden on you, either because you have to personally take care of an aging parent or because this parent is in some sort of nursing facility that is putting a strain on your financial resources.

The added tension that comes from having an aging parent under your wing can, naturally, put a strain on your relationship. You may have imagined that your retirement years were going to be free of such worldly cares, and suddenly you find yourselves spending hours taking care of a parent.

There's a range of emotions that this is likely to trigger. You may feel resentful, guilty, sad, and even a bit afraid when you begin to consider that you may be in the same boat one day. You can't stifle emotions, nor should you; it's unhealthy to try to push strong emotions like these away. If you turn yourself into a stone, emotionally speaking, you'll also end up not being able to feel the love you have for your spouse. But feeling an emotion momentarily and wallowing in it are two different things. When you start to feel one of these emotions, allow yourself a minute or two to process the emotion and then move on. Don't let yourself get trapped into feeling guilty or sad or angry (or a combination of all of them) 24/7. All this will do is leave you no room for the necessary emotions like love and lust that you should be sharing with your partner.

And you're also going to have to be a little selfish. You need some time off from such issues. I'm not going to tell you that you should put an older parent in a nursing home so you can have all the time you need to go play. That decision will be a blend of necessity, compassion, and finances. But if you've taken on the responsibility to care for an older person, you have to also make time to keep your own relationship from being weakened by these duties. The parent may complain about having someone else there to care for them, or of being left alone for a while, but it's important you do this for the sake of your physical, emotional, and sexual health.

Financial difficulties

At the beginning of this chapter I warned you I wasn't a financial advisor, and I haven't gotten an MBA since I wrote that. But financial difficulties are always accompanied by psychological issues, so I do want to touch on this subject.

Everyone has a different way of handling monetary issues, so it's rare both halves of a couple think exactly alike when it comes to money matters. But assuming a couple has come to live with each other's habits when it comes to money, this can all change after retirement, when your income will probably tumble a couple of notches.

📌 Tip:

Working on budgets and communicating on other challenges a couple faces is hard work. Plan to reward yourselves afterwards with a passionate lovemaking session. Knowing you have this planned will make the hard work easier to get through. Or, if you prefer, start with the lovemaking session. With each of you basking in the afterglow of sex, compromises are likely to be easier to arrive at.

The person used to spending money more freely may bristle at the thought of having to suddenly worry about even small amounts. And the person who has always been worried about not having enough money, no matter how much they as a couple actually had, may literally become panicky on this subject.

Some couples have long made a budget and learned to stick with it, and those couples can generally survive without too many problems. But if a household budget was not something you prepared before retirement, I would strongly suggest you work on one now and that you work on it together. This will force you to examine your financial situation and to talk about it. A budget that lists income and expenses will compel the free-spending sort to see, in black and white terms, what is possible and what is not. And the worrier may feel more at ease knowing the couple's life-savings aren't going to run out if they stick to a certain budget. Again, forcing yourselves to communicate honestly will strengthen your relationship, at least once you've come to terms with your finances. However, pretending you'll muddle through without ever really coming to terms with your finances will definitely have a negative effect on your relationship.

This is also a time to start thinking about what is going to happen in the more distant future. The likelihood is one of you will die before the other. One of you may need to go into a nursing home. Your heirs need to be considered. There are tax and legal issues that must be examined, and you'll probably need some experts to point you in the right direction.

After you find out exactly what your options are, talk about them openly and make some decisions. It's always easier to put off such matters, I know, but since you can't predict the future, it's better to face the music and make the right preparations. You don't help your relationship by ignoring the inevitable. You only harm it, especially if you end up fighting over it again and again.

Alcohol – a retirement danger

While retirement is supposed to be a time when there is less pressure on you, as we've seen, sometimes pressure can increase. And even confronting something as simple as boredom can create pressure when it has to be faced day after day. For people who've had a problem dealing with pressure, facing a situation like this can drive them to drink. I know that expression is a cliché, but in this case it is applicable.

There are people who drink moderately all their lives but find themselves leaning more heavily on alcohol when they enter retirement. There's no job to hold on to or other responsibilities to keep them from drinking more than moderately. In some cases, if they're living alone or the spouse is quite busy outside the home, there's no one to notice that they're constantly drunk for days or weeks on end. The problem can grow and grow without any checks.

By the way, an older person's drinking habits don't even have to change to cause a problem. As the body ages, the effects of alcohol may change. The two drinks a man had every evening for decades without showing any effects may actually cause him to become drunk when he's reached retirement age. And certain medications can also amplify the effects of alcohol. (That alcohol can, in turn, have a negative effect on medications is another problem.)

In case you think this isn't a wide-scale problem, a national survey done of people over the age of fifty-fiive in 2002 showed more than six million had engaged in binge drinking (defined as consuming more than five drinks in one session) over the prior thirty days.

Gerontologists are starting to recognize the problem, and there are programs now aimed at helping the elderly who abuse alcohol. The good thing is an older person is more likely to be helped by such a program. So if you or someone you know does have a problem with alcohol, seek out such a program.

Drugs

Many baby boomers gave up their drug use, if they did any, after getting married and having children, but certainly not all did. And similarly to the situation described with regard to alcohol, someone who feels the need to escape could turn to the same drugs they used when they were younger. Because drugs are illegal, and thus harder to obtain, they are not as much of a problem as alcohol, though if an older person is given prescription painkillers, the opportunity for abuse is certainly there. So, as with alcohol, let me urge any older person who has opted to use drugs to be very careful. Your reaction will be different than it once was. The effectiveness of any medication you are taking could be compromised, and you might also fall victim to whomever you get your drugs from, who might think of an older person as easy prey.

The changing role of retirement

The idea of retirement is a relatively new one. In the not too distant past, when people rarely lived to age sixty-five, people would just continue to work at whatever they did for a living until they couldn't do it physically any more. The idea of ceasing to work when you were in good health was completely alien. Then the concept of retirement arose and was quickly embraced as many people didn't want to go on working past a certain age.

Today, the future of retirement is in flux. First of all, as people live longer and longer, the idea that the next generations can afford to support them for twenty or thirty or more years through programs like the United States' Social Security system may not be realistic.

And I'm of the belief that retiring completely is not healthy, at least not for your mental health. So I would guess that in future years, the concept of retirement will change. As it is, people change jobs much more often than they used to, so it's quite possible this will continue with people switching jobs as they get older until they're no longer physically capable of working at all. What this means is, unless you are well into it, your retirement, by the old definition, is not something written in stone.

Even if you could retire in the old sense of the word, it's good to be flexible. The one requirement is to keep up your communication with your partner so you can work out this stage of your life together, with an eye to the outcome being as positive as possible.

10

Second Honeymoons: Firing up the Romance

If you regularly take vacations together, you might be saying to yourself, we don't need a second honeymoon because we've already completed number twenty-one. If you've really gone out of your way to make these vacations romantic, you could be right, and I suggest you skip this chapter.

But going on a honeymoon isn't just like taking a vacation. Certainly most vacations spent with children don't count. And just because the two of you spent a week at a resort doesn't make it a honeymoon, especially if he spent most days playing golf while she shopped and had massages, or you both spent every evening at the casino. These are wonderful activities for a vacation but they don't exactly bring about togetherness. For a second honeymoon, the emphasis has to be on romantic activities done as a couple.

"Hey, Dr. Ruth," some of you are saying right now, "isn't this idea of a second honeymoon silly? We've lived together for decades, so it's not like we just got married and have to learn what it's like to live together. Maybe, in fact, we get too much togetherness. Maybe we need a break from each other."

You say you need a vacation, then I say great. You say you need some time apart during that vacation; I have nothing against that.

But I also say that second honeymoons offer other benefits to your marriage and your relationship that ordinary vacations don't.

And while I'm not saying every vacation or even every other vacation should be like a honeymoon, as the phrase "second honeymoon" implies, going on a purely romantic holiday a decade or two after your marriage is special enough to warrant putting some time, effort, and money into.

You can spend every second of your lives together, living under the same roof and even working together ten hours a day in a cramped office, without ever being romantic. And, careful, when I say being romantic I'm not talking just about having sex. I'm talking about re-cementing the passionate love you had for each other that caused you to get married in the first place.

If your romantic relationship has become a bit stale, you need to put aside a block of time to freshen it up. Certainly a second honeymoon is also a vacation from work and everyday life, but the emphasis of a second honeymoon is on being a couple, not on extraneous activities.

That doesn't mean you have to spend your time on a desert island with absolutely no distractions. You could be exploring some major metropolitan city and still have a very romantic vacation. (I'll be giving you some hints on how to do this in New York City later on.) The same would be true if you were visiting a city you've visited a dozen times. But it won't be a romantic vacation, a second honeymoon, unless you go out of your way to make it into one. You can't just assume because you're on vacation that romance is going to fill the air, even if you're someplace that is very romantic in and of itself. Romance takes a little bit of work.

And while a second honeymoon is undoubtedly going to be a sexy one as well as romantic, don't go thinking that making love every hour on the hour is enough to qualify a vacation as a second honeymoon. First of all, even when you were twenty or thirty years younger you couldn't make love all day and night. And before you go getting all defensive about your current sexual prowess, the point I'm trying to make is that romance is more than just sex. In fact, you can have very passionate sex that is not all that romantic (think of a one-night stand between two strangers) and romantic sex that's not that passionate (think great-grandpa and great-grandma).

So what is this thing we call romance? Here's my definition: Love can't exist in a vacuum. It needs an atmosphere in which to thrive, a medium in which to grow, a place to call home. That atmosphere-medium-place is romance. But romance is delicate, and it takes a lot of thought and planning to insure it is there to nourish your love for each other.

A second honeymoon, or any period of time that is supposed to be romantic, needs to be carefully handled from A to Z. So if A, the first hours of your second honeymoon, begin by you rushing home from work with minutes to spare, followed by a manic throwing about of clothes which you call packing and a mad dash to the airport that ends with you huffing and puffing your way to the gate, winding up with the two of you slumping into your airplane seats and promptly falling asleep, your second honeymoon certainly hasn't gotten off on the right foot. It could take several days to restore yourselves from such a send-off to a mood where romance could actually have a chance of peeking out from behind the dust-cloud of activity.

If you're heading off on your yearly vacation, such a manic departure may be inevitable because often the week before and after a vacation can be so hectic as to make you wonder whether the vacation was worth taking. But if it's your second honeymoon, you have to take every precaution to see that this doesn't happen. You have to plan it so you're home from work early, maybe with some flowers in your hand. You have to pack the night before so you're not rushed. Hopefully you'll have time for a glass of champagne before the car comes to pick you up to pilot you to the airport, during which trip you'll have another glass in the back seat while interlocking knees and staring into each other's eyes. Are you beginning to see the difference?

I understand you can't do that for every vacation, but that's why a second honeymoon isn't just another vacation. And why they're so few and far apart. And why you have to carefully plan so your second honeymoon is a lot more romantic than a mere vacation. Filling the days and nights of a second honeymoon with romance takes extra effort. Yes, you may do some of the regular things you do on a vacation, like sight-seeing and having dinner out, but somehow you have to find a way to make these activities more romantic than they would be on a vacation.

My guess is most of you women readers understand what I'm talking about, but to some of you men this is all a mystery. Of course by saying that, I'm implying romance is something that only women require and know about, but that's not so. You men out there, don't tell me that when you were first falling in love you weren't romantic, even if you weren't all that good at expressing it. If, for example, you drove out of your way to pass by the place where she lived to see if her lights were on, and maybe stopped the car and stared up at her window for a while, that was a very romantic gesture—even if she never knew about it. You were being romantic all for yourself. You might not have done exactly that, but I think you can remember similar starry-eyed things you did when you were falling madly in love.

Do you have any less need for romance now? You might think so, but it's not necessarily true.

Clearly women have a greater need for romance, since they obviously desire it more. Part of the reason for that is physical. As I've discussed in earlier chapters, women take a longer time to become sexually aroused. Ideally for a woman, foreplay would take days, not minutes or seconds. So romance becomes an integral part of foreplay. Young men don't need foreplay; they can become aroused in seconds.

As we go through the years, our lives become so busy, romantic thoughts get pushed aside by everything else to which we tend to give a higher priority. Now remember what I said about older men needing foreplay too. The older a man gets, the longer it takes him to become aroused. Suddenly romance should take on a higher priority as well. But because romance is rather ephemeral, if you don't nurture it, it's hard to create the right aura. The second honeymoon becomes an important opportunity to work together at adding the romance you both need to your relationship. And that one romantic episode can have lasting effects, even years into the future.

Now I don't want any of you guys out there thinking that to suddenly become romantic is a sign of weakness, suggesting you're not as virile as you once were. All we women need is for men to start saying to each other, "Hey look, that guy's acting romantic so that means he's reached the stage where he's having a hard time getting an erection." There's nothing wrong with a man acting romantic mostly for his partner's sake. But I just want to make it clear that it's quite possible for a man to discover that there's a lot more in romance for him than he believed.

And since this book is written for those over fifty, let's also talk about maturity, not in the bad sense but in the good sense. A young man worries about what his pals think of him. Even if he does feel romantic, he may stifle those feelings so as not to get ribbed by his male friends. But if you're over fifty, you should have accomplished enough in your life that such peer pressure should no longer affect you. And maybe you'll find, if you give in to your softer side, that you'll enjoy the emotions you'll tap into. Your relationship with your spouse is much different than it was when you were younger. A lot more water has gone under your common bridge. You have an almost infinite number of connections between the two of you made up of all the memories you've shared. So even if some of the fire has gone out of your sex life, by allowing the emotional connection to grow stronger, you'll be able to strengthen your overall relationship, including the sexual aspects of it. And there's no better way to start this process than by going on a second honeymoon.

Planning makes the difference

So now you're thinking, how exactly do I turn a vacation into a second honeymoon? The biggest difference between the two is the planning. Remember, romance is delicate. If you don't put some effort into creating a romantic atmosphere, it won't necessarily just pop up because you're together. And that's especially true if you're not on your home turf. If you don't know a restaurant, you could end up eating in a place that had a great review for its food but that's packed and plays loud music all the time, hardly an atmosphere where romance can thrive. You want someplace where you can whisper sweet nothings in her ear, so you have to find that place ahead of time and then make reservations. By using the Web, that's pretty easy to do nowadays, but it does require putting in some time and effort.

But here comes one of those silver linings. Planning for a vacation is a way of extending the pleasure. If you're planning for a regular vacation, the two of you can start to picture the fun you'll have. And as you learn more and more about the place you'll be visiting, the anticipation will build and build and the pleasure of your two-week vacation can be extended to several months. The same exact phenomenon can happen when planning a second honeymoon.

Some cautionary words

I need to add a word of caution here. As I've been saying, romance is more ephemeral than other feelings. It's possible to build your expectations too high so that when you experience the real thing, it doesn't measure up. Imagining what the Grand Canyon or the Great Wall of China will look like from seeing pictures is fine because your imagination can't really replace the real thing. But the delicate nature of romance means it can be overwhelmed. If you're too worked up over how romantic a time you're going to have, those emotions can overshadow the real thing, making the experience less romantic. So while I want you to plan out this second honeymoon carefully, and I want you to build up your anticipation to some degree, I don't want you going overboard.

Another cautionary word when it comes to planning a second honeymoon is don't plan for too many activities. Romance calls for a slow moving, leisurely lifestyle. Think in terms sultry and sensuous, not helter and skelter. And there's also the need for some unplanned time gaps so that you can prolong romantic moments when the need or desire arises. If you've planned your schedule so carefully that you're always on a tight deadline, you'll kill the romance, not enhance it. (Hint: stay away from guided tours.)

What's romantic

I met my late husband on the ski slopes. Actually I met him on the ski lift. Because the guy I was with was too tall and we didn't fit together on the T-bar, I picked out this short guy to travel with up the slope. Soon decided it was better to go through life with someone a little closer to my size. Luckily for me, with a little prodding, he agreed. Anyway, since we were both skiers, and since we had a history of having met while skiing even though we never skied down the slopes together because we were at different skill levels, to me a ski vacation was a romantic vacation because of all the memories it included. Now a skiing second honeymoon where you spend the day skiing on different slopes would be counter to everything I've been telling you, right? Of course if you had asked my husband, he would have quoted that old proverb about the shoemaker's children having no shoes. But seriously, you can make any vacation a romantic second honeymoon as long as you're both on the same page.

Where you have to make compromises is when you have different tastes, such as his wanting to play golf and her wanting to sit by the pool. Since he's capable of sitting by the pool and she's not a golfer, it would seem wisest not to choose a resort that has a golf course nearby—but perhaps they could compromise. He could spend some time sitting by the pool with her and she could join him, riding in the cart, while he golfs. But, better yet, it might be wiser to go explore some Andean villages where there are neither golf courses nor pools.

Keeping costs manageable

I should also say a few words here about the cost of a second honeymoon. One thing I don't want you worrying about is how much it is costing you. Worries of any sort can easily put a stop to romance, so by planning a trip that will cost too much, you're setting a trap for yourself. Also, romance sometimes needs some spontaneity, which means you need to have some extra money to splurge once in a while. If you've planned a vacation to the point where every last dime is budgeted for, you could end up with a problem. It is better to set your sights a little lower when, say, reserving hotels or choosing restaurants so that you're not counting pennies when you're actually on this trip.

In any case, I'm never in favor of spending a fortune to make a romantic gesture. That's for people who feel guilty about not being romantic 364 days a year and then go overboard to make up for it. The cost is never justified. If you're planning a trip two months in advance, that gives you plenty of time to put a little extra effort into being a bit more romantic each of the next sixty days. By building up your points in the romance bank, you'll feel less of a need to spend as much on the trip itself. And the more worry-free you are while on this trip—worries about money are very counterproductive when it comes to feeling romantic—the more romantic the trip will be.

Furthermore, sometimes spending too much can backfire. Eat at the fanciest restaurant, ordering everything from soup to nuts, and you might come out feeling bloated. Drink too much of the finest wine or champagne and when you get back to the hotel all you'll want to do is go to sleep. Excess of any sort ends up not being romantic. So better to adopt a middle-of-the-road strategy that can help you to raise the romance quotient to the highest degree.

No time to introduce change

One thing I've said over and over in this book is that you can't change people, and while vacations are actually good opportunities to try to introduce some changes, second honeymoons aren't. Here are some examples.

If one person wants to go on a cruise and the other hates the idea of cruises, you have to stay on dry land. Or if one person likes to camp and the other doesn't, the same thing applies.

On a vacation you should try the native food. You might wind up being served something you hate, but so what, there'll be plenty of other meals. On a second honeymoon nothing is supposed to get in the way of your romance, including food. If one of you gets sick from eating something that he or she isn't accustomed to, or from food that isn't sanitary, this will definitely spoil the evening. And if you break the romantic spirit, you might have problems building it back up again.

Or let's say you love Jacuzzis and your partner doesn't. On a vacation you could ask for a room with a Jacuzzi and hope for the best. A second honeymoon, however, is not the time to throw down challenges. Seeing a Jacuzzi could ruin the romantic aspects of the trip for your partner. So if you know he or she doesn't like Jacuzzis, go out of your way to make sure your room doesn't have one, even if you think the idea of sharing a Jacuzzi would be very romantic.

Compromise is the order of the day because the number one priority is romance. Talk about it; good communication makes for good romance.

Avoid surprise second honeymoons

There's nothing wrong with having some little surprises during a second honeymoon, but I would be against making the whole thing a surprise package. That would put a lot of pressure on your partner. What if you said, "Guess what, next week we're going to Greece!" and next week your husband (or wife) had an important meeting to attend? Even if he could get out of it, knowing that the meeting was taking place back home without him would cause him anxiety and could ruin the honeymoon atmosphere. Since weddings have to be planned way in advance, first honeymoons are also planned way ahead. That should be the case for second honeymoons as well. Remember, you don't go on a second honeymoon every year, the way you do a vacation. This particular trip needs special handling in every aspect.

Even smaller surprises may backfire. Witness Frank and Iris.

Case History: Frank and Iris

Frank and Iris agreed that for their thirtieth wedding anniversary they would go on a cruise to the Caribbean. Iris took up the ball, spending lots of time on the Web finding just the right cruise. She told Frank which islands they'd be stopping at and they agreed on how much they wanted to spend. It seemed nothing could go wrong, as long as a hurricane didn't spring up. But it turned out Iris chose a cruise that was created for people going on second honeymoons. Several hundred people would be sharing the experience with Iris and Frank, including a mass renewal of wedding vows. Iris thought this was a wonderful addition to the cruise. Frank found out as they boarded the ship and hated the concept. He wanted this to be a special time for the two of them. He loathed the idea of being part of a group second honeymoon. Iris' surprise put a damper on the whole trip.

Renewing vows

Since I brought this subject up, let me address it. I don't think renewing vows is a "must do" on a second honeymoon. When you took your vows the first time it was forever, so there's no need to take them again. If this is something you feel strong about, especially if only one of you really wants to do this, I would make it a separate occasion. Why? Because when the topic comes up, each of you is naturally going to conduct an interior review of your marriage. You're going to look at the good and the bad and assess how things went in their entirety, and who knows what your answer is going to be? What if you're on a cruise and the next morning everyone is going to renew their wedding vows, and when you start thinking about it you have a few regrets. Maybe not enough to get divorced, or even to stop you from renewing your vows, but enough to make the moment bittersweet. That kind of review process could remove all traces of romance from this second honeymoon. Remember, no marriage is perfect. The point of a second honeymoon is not to celebrate the past but to make repairs so you can go ahead into the future. So, if renewing your wedding vows carries a risk, maybe you should skip it. I said maybe. It all depends on the couple, but if one of you is hesitant, the other shouldn't insist.

Don't expect perfection

You can't have a perfect second honeymoon. Something is bound to go wrong from time to time. Most vacations are at least somewhat dependent on the weather and that's something you have no control of whatsoever. (Though bad weather can keep you indoors, which may not be all bad.) Be ready to go with the flow. Laugh at adversity. If you get upset because a plane is late or become angry at a surly waiter, you'll add unnecessary tension to your trip, endangering the romantic atmosphere you're trying to maintain.

Honeymoon with a grouch?

There are people who are constantly grouchy. It's their nature to complain and they enjoy it. Couples which include one such partner are going to have a hard time being very romantic. You could ask Oscar the Grouch to tone it down a bit, if only for this trip. Though if it's in his or her nature, I doubt you'll meet with much success.

A personality trait that makes compromise impossible, where one partner insists on having his or her way, will make romance hard to achieve.

If you're the partner of someone like that, you have obviously made some adjustments to your partner's personality, so to you it may be better to have a second honeymoon, even if the romantic quotient is less than ideal.

The same quandary applies to any other personality "quirk" or negative peculiarities such as hypochondria, pessimism, phobias, compulsions, perfectionism, and the like.

There's no one answer to how to handle such issues. It's a subjective matter, and only the people involved can really decide whether it's worth going on a second honeymoon. One piece of advice I can give you in this type of case is that perhaps it might be better for only one of you to go. I know that doesn't make any sense, but listen to me for a second. A grouchy person, to take one example, doesn't usually respond well to pressure. Tell a grouch that he or she is supposed to be especially romantic on this trip and the result is likely to be the opposite of what you want. But what if you didn't tell the other person that this particular vacation was a second honeymoon? What if in planning the trip you added some items that would be romantic for you? For example, if you liked flowers, order some flowers for your room. Or if you were going to a city you'd been to before and there's a restaurant that you find romantic, make reservations to go there. Yes, this second honeymoon would be taking place mostly in your imagination. But you know what? That's better than nothing. And let's face it, second honeymoons aren't always based on reality anyway, as you often must artificially create the romantic atmosphere to the best of your ability. So having a second honeymoon that's half fantasy and half reality could be better than not having one at all. Of course if you're going to get frustrated by this, if having your fantasy burst every two seconds by your grouchy partner is going to make you grouchy, too, then forget that I ever mentioned this idea. In the total scheme of things, having a second honeymoon is not absolutely necessary. That's why I say this is a subjective decision only you can make. On the other hand, if you never thought of it and it makes sense, then try it the next time you go on vacation. And let me know what happens.

Luxury not required

Some of you, especially those who are slightly spoiled, may have said to yourselves, when I suggested going to Andean villages, "How could anyone go to some remote village in the Andes, or any place without a host of luxury amenities, for a romantic second honeymoon?" To you I say, if you're equating luxury with romance, you've missed the boat.

Diamond rings and mink coats and fancy sports cars aren't necessarily romantic gifts. They could be, just as a piece of paper folded into some origami shape could be. It's not the cost that matters, but the thought. If someone gives you an expensive gift because they're feeling bad about how little time they've spent with you, romance isn't the ruling emotion in such an exchange. It's guilt. On the other hand if they're making a financial sacrifice to show their love, that's romantic.

Let's get back to those villages in the Andes. This could be a very romantic setting because the number of distractions would be minimal. There'd be no TV in your bare-bones hotel room. The local restaurant might serve tasty food but the ambience would be primitive. There wouldn't be any nightclubs or theaters or movies to go to afterward. About all you could do would be to sit outside, huddled in a lot of clothes because it's always cold up there, and look at the stars. That, ladies and gentlemen, would be genuinely romantic. It would be just the two of you without any distractions. You'd hold hands. You'd put your arms around each other. You'd talk. You'd get closer. And when you came back from such a trip, you'd have unique new memories to share, and any dents in your relationship would likely have been fully repaired.

I'm not saying you can't have a romantic second honeymoon in Las Vegas, but I am saying it would be a lot harder to achieve. If you want to go someplace and forget about life back home, the more distractions the better. And what has more distractions than Las Vegas? No place on earth. But distractions are exactly what you don't want when you're trying to focus on each other and be romantic.

In reality, most people would prefer, and would do best, planning their second honeymoon in a place that offers more things to see and do than a remote mountain-top village and yet fewer things than the hectic, twenty-four-hour glitter of Las Vegas.

Destination New York

It's a big world out there and I'm not writing a travelogue here. But to give you a bit more guidance, I decided to give you some ideas from my hometown of New York City. There's certainly an abundance of places to stay, eat, and visit in the Big Apple, but I hope by giving you a few examples you'll have a better understanding of how to pick and choose among the available attractions with an eye to enhancing the romantic content of your trip. (Keep in mind that each couple is different and that some might not find these places as romantic as others.)

New York has many fine, large hotels like the Waldorf and the Plaza. They're great hotels, but they're so big that they end up being impersonal. You want to feel special while on a second honeymoon, and it's difficult to do that when staying at a large hotel. There are also what are called "boutique" hotels. There's one I'm familiar with, The Library Hotel, because they dedicated an entire room to me. Each room in this hotel has a different theme based on the Dewey Decimal system. One is a Love Room, with several of the books I've written. But the point isn't to go there and read my books. The fact that it's small means the staff will quickly get to know you. You'll feel special, which is how you should feel when on a second honeymoon. There are many boutique hotels in New York and other big cities. In Germany and other European countries, these small hotels abound. In the more rural areas and smaller cities of the United States and Canada, you may find quaint "bed and breakfasts." In my opinion, you should choose one of these smaller, more intimate accommodations for this type of trip.

The restaurant I think is the most romantic in the city is The Sea Grill. This fine restaurant overlooks the skating rink at Rockefeller Center. It's one story below ground level so, during the winter, the ice skaters are directly in front of you. There you are in the heart of Manhattan gazing out at this special little world of circling skaters. You know how lovers like to sit gazing into a fireplace, watching the different shapes of the flames? This has the same effect. Other restaurants that have something similar to offer are the Four Seasons, where there's a pool in the main dining room, and Aquavit, which has a waterfall.

What I'm saying here is to look for a place that has good food, obviously, but also one that has something about its ambience that makes it a bit special and that you can lose yourself in. If you're spending a week or ten days together on this second honeymoon, there are going to be quiet moments when you don't want to talk. It's nice to have something serene to contemplate like a fountain or a fireplace, or even just the quiet buzz of efficient waiters. And be sure to shun those restaurants with multiple TVs, each featuring a different sporting event. What you want is something that adds to your romantic sensory experience, not something that offers sensory overload.

Of course there are also going to be times when you want to dine without any distractions except each other. One obvious choice is room service, where you can dine in personal seclusion dressed in as little as you wish. Also keep in mind that many Japanese restaurants have what they call tatami rooms, which are in the back and walled off. They may require you to spend a certain amount of money to reserve one. They're usually for large groups, but if you go to a restaurant on a quiet night, you might be able to get one set aside just for the two of you, especially if you let them know this is a special occasion.

Tip:

Wherever you eat while on your second honeymoon, be careful not to eat or drink to excess. Your whole vacation is to be savored, which means taking small portions, whether food or sights or lovemaking and slowly probing and experiencing each so you get the most out of every morsel.

Oh, yes, I want you to put diets on the back burner—if possible. Obviously if you have allergies or are a diabetic, you have to remain careful. But while I'm telling you not to eat so much that you feel bloated or lethargic, this doesn't mean you should be counting calories either. Instead, look for foods you genuinely love and count as experiences. If some are high in calories, so be it. You're on your second honeymoon.

And of all the sights I could recommend in New York, I'm going to highlight one that is actually very close to where I live: The Cloisters. It's part of the Metropolitan Museum, but it's a separate entity up at the northern tip of Manhattan. The building materials were all brought over from Europe, though not from only one place, and it looks a bit like a small castle. The point is that it's a smaller museum with lots of small spaces to explore. So, for the most part, you're never overwhelmed by either the exhibits or the crowds. It's a place where you can lose yourself a bit and feel like it's your special art gallery. You won't feel out of place holding hands or putting your arms around each other; in fact, I believe that when walking around this museum, you actually feel drawn into this type of closeness and touching. And be sure to explore the park around it too, Fort Tryon and the Heather Gardens. If you look closely, you'll find a bench dedicated to my late husband, Fred Westheimer.

Wherever you go on your second honeymoon, seek out the smaller, less busy, more intimate attractions, so you can feel the two of you are a part of the experience rather than just observers.

Shopping

I know shopping is the great American pastime, but it's not terribly romantic. The most unromantic part is when it forces you to have an agenda. If you have to get a gift for this one and that one, that's going to put pressure on you. One way of avoiding this is shopping ahead of time. See if you can't go online and find some gifts from where you're going and order them so they'll be waiting for you at home. Your relatives will never know, and you'll be left to concentrate on each other instead of shopping for others. But if you must do some shopping, again use the Web to look up exactly where you should go. Try not to waste time hopping in and out of every shop you see. If you have one or two destinations, you can shop using your time as efficiently as possible.

That doesn't mean you shouldn't shop for yourselves. Let's say you have a space on the living room wall that you'd like to fill, and so you decide to visit some art galleries to see if anything appeals to you. That type of shopping does have a romantic aspect to it, particularly if you can find just the right piece of artwork which remionds you got it on your second honeymoon each time you look at it forever after. But try to avoid shopping for personal items you could just as easily get at home, like shoes or shirts.

The second honeymoon schedule

I'm going to suggest that in order to make this second honeymoon special, you vary your usual schedule. Some days get up later than you normally would and just languish in bed; on other days arise early and watch the sunrise over lattes. If you're used to eating dinner at 6:00 P.M., eat later or earlier on some nights, or even skip dinner and have a huge breakfast the next day. Or have a large lunch and a small snack for dinner. A visit to a deli and a picnic on a park bench can be especially romantic. Some restaurants offer specially priced "early-bird" dinners served before the crowds arrive. These dinners offer not only a chance to save a bit of money, but, since the restaurant is less crowded, a bit more intimacy. Mix it up so every meal is a little special.

Mixing things up especially applies to the times when you have sex. You may have sex usually in the late evening, but on this second honeymoon, try the mornings, the afternoons, before dinner, after breakfast. Not only will such variety spice things up, but you might find that you enjoy having sex at one of these other times much better and continue the practice at home. And there might be other advantages as well. If you have sex before dinner, it matters less if you eat a heavy meal and split a bottle of wine that causes you to fall right asleep when you get back to the hotel.

Don't forget to try a naked dinner using room service. Order foods that don't have to be eaten hot, salads and such, and try to stretch the whole experience out, alternating mouthfuls of food with kisses and strokes.

And since I've brought up sex, it's time to talk about expanding your sexual repertoire. Try some positions you've never used. If one or two don't work, well, you can always go back to the tried and true. But this would be a good time to experiment, though it isn't a good time to put pressure on your partner if he or she doesn't want to explore in a certain direction. In fact, you might want to talk about which positions and what things to try ahead of time. That way you're both on the same page.

Don't have sex only in bed. Be careful not to hurt yourself, but look around and see what each place where you stay has to offer with regard to adding some variety to your second honeymoon sex life. Are there deserted beaches? Does your hotel room have an over-sized shower? If you have a suite, is there a comfortable couch where you could make love while watching an erotic pay-for-view movie?

Whatever you do, don't scrimp on the foreplay. I'm not talking about touching her left breast when you're already in bed. I mean when you're looking at a window display, take her into your arms and kiss her. When you're walking down a street, make sure you're touching in some way. Give each other a massage in the shower. When you're in a cab, put your hand on his or her knee. It doesn't matter when you're actually going to have sex, but touch each other as often as possible so, when you do have sex, all this foreplay will have had time to work.

Sex without orgasms

During your normal busy lives, if you're together naked, touching each other, stroking each other, and having intercourse, you're both going to want to have an orgasm, because after all, they're not available all that often. But, if you're on a second honeymoon, you can stop lovemaking before experiencing an orgasm, do something else for a while, and, if the mood strikes, come back to it an hour later. Or ten minutes later.

I'm not suggesting you try this on the first day of this honeymoon. At that point you should be actively craving each other, and you're not going to want to stop. But after three or four days of having sex and orgasms one, two, or more times a day, your level of satiety should be pretty high, and you could stop without it being uncomfortable.

Why should you stop? Actually you should tell each other ahead of time that, during this lovemaking session, you're not trying to have orgasms. (If by chance you do anyway, don't worry, there's no penalty.) The point is to enjoy all these pleasures—kissing, touching, licking, having intercourse —in and of themselves. When you're doing these activities waiting for the Big O, naturally they all end up playing second fiddle. You're anticipating this tremendous jolt of pleasure, so how much are you really paying attention to the sensory tingles of every little kiss? But when you know ahead of time that there isn't going to be an orgasm, when there's no clock ticking, so to speak, you can focus more on what you're actually doing. This is especially true if you're having intercourse. You'll be able to make a much closer examination of the sensations caused by his penis slipping in and out of her vagina.

When you're done, and remember you can take as long as you like because there's no official end to this process, you may say that was nice but I'd prefer having an orgasm. Or else you may find a new appreciation for orgasm-less sex. You may want to try it again once you're home.

As men get older, they may find they have more and more difficulty reaching an orgasm. Sometimes after engaging in sex, in its various and sundry forms, for a while they may just say to their partner, "Let's stop, because I know this isn't going to work." And the same thing could happen to many older women. Now if you've practiced this form of sex when an orgasm was quite possible but voluntarily skipped, you'll have a better appreciation for doing so when it's not voluntary. You'll understand that you don't have to feel frustrated by not having an orgasm. Even without an orgasm, sex offers lots of different types of pleasures. What spoils such instances of orgasm-less sex is the pressure. If you're trying hard to have a climax and don't, it's natural to feel disappointed. But if you've practiced this type of sex before, then maybe after a bit of lovemaking you can say to your partner, "I'm not going to have an orgasm, but let's not stop, let's enjoy each other without having an orgasm." And you'll both understand that "orgasm-less sex" isn't an oxymoron, but that it's actually pleasurable.

I hope you now have a new appreciation for second honeymoons. As you have seen, they're different from a plain vacation, but that's what makes them special. They're definitely worth pursuing because the result should be that your relationship is further solidified.

11

Finding a Partner

So far in this book I've been speaking to couples, or at least to individuals who are part of a couple, probably married but not necessarily so. But, of course, that leaves out a large segment of the over-fifty population. While most people do marry at some point in their lives, half of all marriages entered into in the United States end in divorce. Partners die, and some people choose never to tie the knot, so a large group of the over-fifty crowd are single.

Single at the moment or not, most people over fifty want to have a steady partner whom they can rely on for companionship as well as to share physical pleasure. Of course some singles in this age group decide for one reason or another that they don't want a regular partner. Those people needn't read this chapter, skipping right to the next one, which I'm sure they will find more beneficial. The biggest problem people over fifty face, or to be honest, women over fifty, has to do with demographics. Women live longer than men; so the older a woman is, the fewer men there are to choose from. And, since many of the men already have a partner, the pool of available single men is even smaller. On top of this, men tend to look for younger women and this makes the pool smaller yet. This is especially true when a woman gets beyond her sixties. Just because the numbers make it somewhat difficult for an older woman to find a single male to date, it is far from impossible. And, if she has the right attitude, she can even make the process of locating one enjoyable and successful.

There are also men who, despite the better odds, also have difficulty finding a partner; so this chapter is for all singles over fifty.

What singles want

The American Association of Retired Persons did a survey of singles over fifty to find out what their thoughts were about dating. On the one hand I'm not a big fan of surveys because unless they are very carefully done, their results can be skewed. But since this isn't an issue of life or death, I thought I'd pass along a few of the results I found interesting, especially some cases that offer what are called "teachable moments," the definition of which I think you'll quickly see.

According to this survey of 3,500 single men and women aged forty to sixty-nine, almost 60 percent of the men felt their frequency of sex was not enough, while only 35 percent of women felt that way. And even among those who were in a steady dating relationship, 48 percent of the men said they weren't getting enough sex, compared to 33 percent of the women.

What's the explanation for this discrepancy between men and women? First of all, since men's egos are tied into their sexual prowess, there is a natural inclination to brag in this area. So do the men who complain about not getting enough sex all really feel that way? My guess is many say that just because it's expected of them. The logic goes something like: "I'm a real man and real men need a lot of sex, so how can I possibly be getting enough?"

Certainly the single men whose partners are complaining about not getting enough sex aren't admitting that they are falling down on the job. How can I be so sure? Because when you add up the percentages, that would mean only a small fraction of single people thought their sex life was adequate, and I doubt that's true.

Now we're not all the same, and I'm not saying there aren't plenty of people in every age bracket who aren't satisfied with the number of times they have sex. But is that difference in sexual appetite as large as this survey makes it seem? In my opinion, I don't believe these results accurately reflect the reality of the situation.

Surveys or no surveys, here's what's important for you: What other people do has absolutely no bearing on your needs and wants. How often to engage in sex is an area of a relationship where it is easy to start fights, and both sides can use the statistics from this survey, or any other they may read, to back up their argument. But the important point is that if you're in a relationship where you're engaging in sex and you're mature adults, not teenagers, then you should be able to work out a compromise.

Both men and women are free to masturbate if they're feeling sexually frustrated, and both men and women can give their partner sexual satisfaction even if they don't want to take an active part in a sexual encounter or have an orgasm themselves. So every couple's sex life should be a mixture of mutual sex, sex where only one partner gets sexual satisfaction, and masturbation.

The exact mix has to be decided by the partners in question, but don't pretend you have equal sex drives, because undoubtedly you don't. That inequality shouldn't matter as long as you take the right attitude.

What a survey like this really shows is even among people in this age bracket, there are far too many who are what I call sexually illiterate. One partner feels he or she isn't getting enough sex, and the two of them can't figure out a way to satisfy both of them. To me, that is the significance of this particular survey.

To arrive at a balance that works for both partners is important for married people, but even more important for singles. Married people, particularly those who have been married a long time, have many bonds. Single people who are dating have many fewer ties. That gives the place sex takes in their relationship more importance, and so it's much more likely for sexual frequency to become an impediment among singles who are dating. It's certainly true when two people are first getting involved sexually. Their level of arousal is going to be higher, but that still doesn't mean each will have an identical level of desire. There will be some differences, and those have to be handled properly if the relationship is to thrive.

There's another set of factors that also have to be taken into account the older both partners are: Sex isn't the same for older people as it is for younger people. He may have to take a pill in order to get an erection. She may need a lubricant to allow for penetration. And they both may have assorted aches and pains that have to be dealt with. In other words, they're going to have to communicate better and be more forthright about any problems they may have in order to have sex at all.

That's not necessarily a bad thing. As we talked about, it may sound absurd to say that two people, of any age, having sex aren't intimate, but there are different levels of intimacy among sexual partners. Greater intimacy can mean better sex. So two people who are forced to share their problems will end up being more intimate and they may find this improves their overall enjoyment of the sexual experience. Here's an example.

Case History: Bob and Louise

Bob lost his wife to cancer the year he retired. A couple of years later he began to feel that he would be comfortable dating and joined a senior center. There he met Louise, who was a couple of years older than he was but very energetic. The second he'd walked in the door, she'd spotted him as a potential partner, and no one else at the center had a chance once she'd set her mind to it.

After dating for a month, it was clear to both of them they were going to have sex. As they each waited for their next date, they were both quite aroused thinking about the prospects. Bob's wife had been very conservative, and their sex life had been routine and not very fulfilling for Bob. He experienced quite a different set of circumstances with Louise.

When Bob's wife had gone through menopause, she'd been reticent to use a lubricant. Instead she'd let Bob have intercourse, but she insisted he get it over with quickly so she wouldn't get sore. And at that point she'd stopped trying to have orgasms any more. Louise, on the other hand, was quite open about her sexuality. She didn't try to hide her body at all, in fact flaunted it; had no hesitation to perform oral sex on Bob to help him get an erection, and when it came time to apply a lubricant, did it with such gusto that it became part of the entire sexual experience. Afterwards Bob admitted he hadn't had such an exciting time in decades.

Of course older adults have to be willing to get over that intimacy obstacle in the first place. Older singles may encounter several roadblocks to intimacy. The first has to do with their upbringing. The sexual revolution may have started in the 1960s, but it didn't spread uniformly; so while many older people lived through that era, that doesn't mean they were equally affected by it. Many retained the identical sexual values of the preceding generation.

For someone with a conservative set of values, whose first and only sex partner was their spouse, to suddenly find themselves single can pose many difficulties. This is especially true for anyone who still believes sex should only occur after marriage, a notion that doesn't quite jibe with most of today's singles scenes.

If a woman decides ahead of time that she won't have sex with a man until they're married, and many of the other single women her age don't share that ideal, she's going to have a hard time competing with the Louises of the world. Even if she decides she might be willing to let that particular value slide, she may lack some of the technical skills.

Warning: It's time for a warning, which I may repeat a few more times in this chapter. Remember, just because you're older doesn't mean you have no need to fear getting a sexually transmitted disease. Where condoms may not be necessary to prevent an unintended pregnancy within a circle of people who are all past menopause, that doesn't mean they may not be needed to prevent the spread of disease. Now older men, who may already have some difficulties obtaining an erection, may balk at the idea of using condoms. That's okay as long as they've been recently tested for STDs.

I know many older women are going to give up on this ideal. If they've found an available male after looking for a long time, they may just take their chances. I recognize that, but I still have a duty to warn you. I'm going to give you some more advice on this matter later in this chapter.

So how might you deal with a set of values that keeps you from getting the companionship you need? First of all, if this is based on religious values, looking for a partner who shares your religion might be very helpful.

If it is more personal, the best advice I can give you is to try to be flexible. If you go into the dating scene with a chip on your shoulder, saying to yourself and maybe even to others something like, "I will not sleep around," that attitude will be felt by others. But if you keep an open mind, perhaps you'll find someone who'll be able to change it for you. You might meet someone who will sweep you off your feet, and you won't regret giving up the values you held. I'm not telling you that you should or shouldn't have sex with anyone, only not to make up your mind until you're at that bridge when it needs to be crossed.

Problems with body image

Another obstacle to intimacy among singles is that old bugaboo, body image. Many married people encounter difficulties exposing themselves to someone they know quite well—their spouses. But, if you have a lack of confidence in the way you look, taking your clothes off in front of a person you don't know all that well can be even more intimidating.

My first tip about this issue to anyone who has this problem is to get more comfortable with your own body. You live alone, so stop covering up and spend time in the house naked. Pull down the shades and leave a bathrobe by the door so if someone rings you can quickly cover up.

I also want you to spend some time looking at yourself naked in the mirror. Let's suppose you have a potbelly or a scar you don't like. If you never look at it, when you do see it, perhaps stepping out of the shower, you're going to shrink away from that part of your body. You're going to feel ashamed of it. But if you look at it every day, you'll get more used to it. And the less ashamed you are of it yourself, the less ashamed you'll be in front of someone else.

Something else you could do is join a club or gym where you have the opportunity to take your clothes off. I'm not asking you to become a nudist. I mean, let's say there is a pool nearby. Force yourself to go swimming, and when you change in the locker room, don't do it quickly in some corner when no one is looking. Take your time and parade around naked a bit. I don't want you to overdo it and embarrass anyone else, but make a point of doing it enough to help you overcome some of the shyness you may feel. It will also be helpful to take a look around at the other bodies you see, and you'll probably feel better about your own body.

And if you really have some serious problems, do something about it. If you need to lose some weight, go on a diet. If you have a bad scar, maybe a plastic surgeon could help you. I'm sure you try to look your best when you're in a situation where you might meet somebody of the opposite sex, so what's the point of that if you let the body under your clothes go to pot.

And keep in mind, your partner is likely to have some age-related flaws that show up when he or she lets the robe drop. In fact, a would-be partner is probably a bit apprehensive for the same reasons you are. So, given this, what would be a good tool to bring into play? Yep, you guessed it: communication. How about you starting it off with a comment like, "You know I'm not exactly the same svelte, dashing figure I was at twenty-five" and see where it goes. You'll probably find the ice broken with the other person admitting he or she isn't either.

Fear of failure

If you were in a long-running relationship, and something happened one night that prevented you from having sex, you could laugh it off because you'd successfully had sex many, many times before and would do so again. But when having sex for the first time with someone, any such problems can become amplified. And worse than the actual problem can be the fear that it will reoccur.

Sexual functioning is very delicate. Yes, once you're at the point when an orgasm is imminent, there's no stopping it. But before you reach that point of sexual arousal, your libido can become derailed. Let's say a man tried to have sex and lost his erection in the middle of the encounter. The next time he was going to have sex, he would be likely to worry that the same thing would happen. This worry alone could cause him to lose his erection again, turning the problem into a vicious cycle.

If you find yourself in such a situation, there's one important rule that you have to remember: Forget about your problem and make sure that your partner gets sexual satisfaction. If your partner doesn't walk away sexually frustrated, then the likelihood is he or she is not going to think what happened was significant with regard to the relationship. But if your failure causes you to stop the process and withdraw from this other person, this new partner is going to feel as frustrated as you are.

This person may give you another chance, but the pressure will only be stronger the next time, making it more likely that the problem will crop up again. The way to avoid such an occurrence is to relieve as much pressure from the situation as possible, and making sure your partner is sexually satisfied is one way of doing that.

Of course that's just a temporary patch. If the problem is one that needs medical attention, such as with a man who needs a pill to maintain his erections, then he must go get help. If a woman suddenly finds that she's not lubricating enough to allow for penetration, she has to be prepared with some artificial lubricant. And if one of you has a problem, with arthritis, for example, and can only use certain positions, you have to have an open discussion so you're both on the same page. Trying to play hero and attempting sexual positions that are going to cause you pain will undoubtedly result in failure.

If you're not sure which positions will work best, exploring can be part of the fun and also very arousing. It all depends on your attitude. So, if you have a problem, try to see the light side. Don't make a mountain out of a molehill. You can adjust the perspective of this partner with your attitude. If you make it seem like a big problem, this partner is likely to think it is. But if you can laugh it off, your partner will adopt the same attitude.

Learning from your mistakes

What if, for some reason, perhaps sexual, perhaps not, a particular dating relationship fails. For whatever reason, the two of you don't click. As the saying goes, don't cry over spilled milk. If the relationship wasn't meant to be, so be it. But that doesn't mean you should completely forget about it. There's a good chance that there are some lessons in a failed relationship that you need to heed so the next one goes better.

Tip:

If in your lifetime you've gone from one bad relationship to the next, in a never-ending series, there's a good chance you're doing something wrong. Perhaps you don't know how to choose partners. Or your self-esteem is so low you can't hold on to partners. Whatever the problem is, it's probably serious enough to warrant professional help. Go to a professional counselor and lay it on line, being as honest as possible and not blaming the other party each and every time. Hopefully the therapist will spot whatever is causing this trend and help you correct it.

What if the problem is sexual in nature? Let's say you're a man and you had difficulties maintaining your erection. Certainly you're going to have the same worries with a new partner. What you must do is try to address this problem before you go out looking for someone new. In this particular case, what you may need to do is see a doctor and find out whether Viagra or a similar drug would be the proper response. Or, if some medicine you're taking is the problem, whether your doctor would allow you to adjust the dosage. Just by taking some action, you'll gain some added confidence and reduce the possibility of the problem reoccurring because, as I've said, the psychological component of such problems is often quite strong.

Another lesson you might draw from a past mistake is examining how you handled it. If you were clumsy about it and made the other person feel uncomfortable, you know you have to do better. Let's say you're a woman who has a bad back and it is important for your partner not to put all his weight on you. Maybe with a previous partner you didn't say anything up front, but when you started wincing with pain, that put an end to having sex. Or maybe you communicated the problem in a way that turned your partner off. What I suggest you do is to practice how you're going to handle this the next time. Write down some things you might say. Repeat them in front of a mirror. Use humor. You might even be able to use it to arouse a future partner.

How would you do that? Let's say while you're having dinner, you manage to say something about your back: "These chairs are really comfortable, they're good for my poor aching back." Your date is going to respond in some way, and then you say, "It's part of growing older, I guess, but I don't really let it stop me from doing anything. For example, when having sex, I know it's so much better on a hard floor for me than on a soft bed, and I just let my partners know in advance." Now this dinner date (whom I assume at this point you find attractive) is going to be picturing the two of you having sex on the floor, which he will find arousing. Whatever he was thinking about you, he will now add a sexual quotient too. And he'll know that if he does manage to have sex with you, he has to be careful about your back. So you see, you'll have communicated several important messages in preparing the way in this manner.

Preparing to find a partner

This chapter is titled "Finding A Partner," and obviously you can't be having sex with anyone if you haven't met anyone yet. So one key to successful dating is meeting people in the first place. Here's some advice on how to do that.

The most important advice about this I can give you may seem ridiculously obvious, but you'd be surprised how many people need to hear it: Get out of the house. Every minute you spend at home is a minute that you have almost no hope of finding someone, unless you happen to be meeting people via the Internet. Even then, since it isn't safe to invite someone you meet this way into your house until you get to know him or her, you'll have to get out of the house to meet the person.

Therefore, the higher the priority you place on finding a partner, the more time you should spend away from the comfort of your nest. Even with going for a walk around the block, the likelihood of meeting someone is greater than sitting at home. So if you don't do anything else, go for regular walks in the neighborhood, though admittedly that's probably not going to be enough.

Before I move on, however, let me say something about these walks that also applies to many other situations. It's not enough to just put on your walking shoes or sneakers and start walking. You have to prepare for this walk and you have to walk differently than if you were actually just getting exercise.

Preparations include your manner of dress and what else you bring with you. What should you wear? It doesn't matter to me, but it has to be provocative. By that I don't mean you need to show a lot of skin. What I do mean is that you have to look your best and be wearing something that will get you noticed by the other sex. If you're a woman, all it might take is adding a bright pink scarf to the outfit.

Or a man could wear a light colored hat. Or he could carry a decorative cane. And she could have a boomerang in her hand. "A boomerang?" you're saying. Yes, not because she's going to throw it but because it would be a great conversation opener. People are bound to spot it and ask her about it. And she should have a great story to go with it. That way, if she happens to see a guy she thinks might be eligible, she has something to attract him to that initial conversation.

Now I said a boomerang only because it's a fun word. It can be anything, as long as it is an attention getter. The other day I was walking in Central Park and I saw a man with a large yellow snake around his shoulders. Boy, was he getting stopped. I'm not saying you have to go that far, but if the only prop you have is a little zipper pouch with your keys in it hanging around your belly, making it look bigger than it really is, you might as well walk up and down your hallway at home for all the good it will do you in meeting someone of the opposite sex.

And as soon as you start your walk, I want your mind engaged in the process of looking for a date. First of all, you have to smile at the people you pass. That will put you in the right mood for meeting somebody, and one of those smiles you flash could be at someone who will end up being your next date.

Be friendly with everyone. Even if a person you meet is the wrong sex or way too young or way too anything to be a potential partner, he or she might have a friend or a relative they might end up introducing to you.

You also have to be prepared with interesting topics of conversation. If you listened to the news before you left, you should have some ideas. You can rehearse them, silently, as you walk. The night before you may have read an interesting magazine article or looked up something on the Web that would make good conversation. Don't assume you'll think of something when the time comes. You might find yourself tongue-tied and miss an opportunity to show someone what a fascinating person you really are.

This advice is not only for your walks but for anytime you are out of the house. You should always have a prop handy (though a boomerang might not be appropriate in a china shop) and you should always have something prepared in the way of a conversation opener. Opportunity does strike, sometimes in the strangest places, and you must always be prepared. This is especially true for older women who are facing stiff competition and who can't count on a short skirt doing the trick. Better to face the facts and do whatever is necessary than pretend you don't have these obstacles to overcome and let them get the better of you.

Activities

Taking part in activities is another common method for meeting people. What I want to add is that you should choose these activities both for the potential to meet someone new and to make productive use of your time. In other words, if you like studying art history, join a group that visits local museums. Even if you don't find a partner, you'll have had the opportunity to go to museums, which you like to do anyway.

Obviously you have to use a little common sense when choosing activities that are going to help you find a partner. If you're a woman who likes to crochet and all the outside activities you partake in involve crocheting, which is guaranteed to draw in an almost exclusively female crowd, you have to expand your horizons a bit to include activities that men enjoy. This doesn't mean that you have to go to football games (though that's not a terrible idea, as there are certainly a lot of men at sporting events and not many single women to compete against). It just means you have to look at two sides of any activity, the enjoyment you'll get out of it and its potential as a source of meeting someone of the opposite sex.

📌 Tip:

Perhaps you've noticed, a number of times in this book I've mentioned the negative effect a man's interest in golf can have on a relationship. Now here's where you women might turn the tables and use this to your advantage. Golf courses are full of men, many of them single and your age. And many of these men would love to hook up with a woman who would play golf with them. While golf is a tough sport to get good at, it isn't a sport that takes peak physical conditioning. Many men and women play golf well into their eighties and beyond. Check it out. You might find two things to become passionate about: a man and a hobby. tennis ?

Should you go alone or with a friend?

It might make sense to get some friend of yours to join you in whatever activity your choose. You could travel there and back together, and you would have a constant source of companionship. But there is a downside to this. If you're there with a friend, you're going to have to talk to this friend. You won't be as free to go up to someone of the opposite sex. And vice versa—someone of the opposite sex might be intimidated from approaching you.

I don't have a hard and fast answer for you with regard to this question. Going alone might mean being bored or feeling awkward. Going with someone might negate an opportunity to meet someone. So the decision will depend on the activity. Let's say you're going on these museum tours I mentioned earlier. Everyone on the tour will be interested in art, so even if you don't meet someone of the opposite sex, you should meet many other people who share similar interests, be they other single people of your sex or couples. So in a situation like that, I think you could safely go by yourself. But if you were going to a onetime event which might not have anyone interesting, you might decide you'd prefer not to go alone.

While I'm not telling you what to do, I do urge you to be a bit more daring than you normally are. You're on a mission, to find a partner, and that has to take some priority. If you always take the safe road, the odds of your finding someone will go down, and then you won't be able to satisfy the yearning for companionship that you have. Since the reward could be great, and the danger—really mainly of boredom—the more places you go alone, the more likely you will meet someone interesting.

Picky, picky, picky

Once a young lady I knew came to visit me to ask me to introduce her to this famous comedian. He was *the* person she wanted to date and no one else would do. First of all, I couldn't help her, but even if I could have made the introduction, it would likely have been futile. He could have nearly any woman he wanted. For her to put all of her eggs into one basket was a recipe for remaining single, not to say anything about heartbreak and frustration.

Young people put a lot of importance on looks. But they're immature, so you might expect them to make a mistake like that. But you're more mature. You should have learned by now that people of every stripe have something to offer and that you shouldn't limit your search to the narrow band of the population that would make good models.

And I don't want you to think of this as "lowering your sights." I still want you to aim high; I just want you to aim at a broader range of characteristics. I want you to think positive. When you meet someone who is single, stop looking at what is wrong with this person—after all, no one is perfect, even you—and look at what's good about him or her.

Now it's certainly possible someone could have one overriding negative quality that would make you never want to spend more than thirty seconds with that person. I understand that. But rather than make a quick judgment based on a superficial flaw, I want you to look a little deeper. Assume the glass is half full rather than half empty. Remember, all I'm talking about here is going out on a date. If you were going to marry someone, I would be the first one to tell you to examine the other party pretty closely. but for dating purposes, be somewhat lenient.

This advice does depend on your situation. If you have plenty of people to select from, you can be a little pickier. But if you only go on dates once in a while, to increase your dating quotient, you have to be more open-minded. You'll also find that the more dates you go out on, the easier it will be, the better you'll be at the dating game and the more dates you'll get. Why will you get more dates? Because the word will go around that you are willing to date. Somehow other single people of the opposite sex will learn this and your phone will ring.

Tell the world

Letting people know you want to be asked out on dates is crucial to being successful. The more people know, and I mean relatives, friends, neighbors, the person from whom you buy your newspaper in the morning, the better your chances.

Is this a bit embarrassing? Yes it is. You're admitting you can't find a partner all on your own. You're saying to everyone, "I need help." But as someone who gives help professionally, I say that you have to learn to say that. When people ask me a question about some problem, I tell them they've made the most important step. By asking for help, you're much more likely to find help. However, by pretending you don't need help when you do, you're putting yourself in a situation where you probably won't succeed. You might, but the odds are a lot less. So let the world know you want to go out on dates and see what develops.

Using computers

Literally millions of single people are using the Internet to look for a partner. A good many of them have been successful, some even finding future spouses that way. I have to be perfectly honest right here and say there was no one more skeptical about this when it first began than I. I'm not good with technology and the idea of meeting someone without first seeing their face just didn't make any sense to me. I would still say the best way of meeting someone is face to face, but with so much evidence that meeting people via computer can work, I've been forced to admit I was wrong.

There are some safety issues, but the numbers, again, make this way of meeting people, when done with a couple of safeguards in place, not much more risky than meeting someone in person. There are creeps out there, there's no doubt about it, but there aren't millions of them, and there are millions of people using the Web. So the odds are with you rather than against you, as they once were.

I have two pieces of advice to give you. The first is always insist on meeting face-to-face, at least the first time, in a public place. Second, make sure you let other people, either friends or relatives, know you're meeting people on the Internet, and let anyone that you start making contact with know that this interaction is not a closed loop. If you say something like "I told my sister about you and she thought you sounded interesting," then this person will know he can't totally hide if he were to try to harm you in some way. Look at giving up some of your privacy as a form of insurance.

Since I'm not an expert on computer dating, and I want you to be as safe as possible, I decided to look at the largest site for Internet dating, Match.com, to see what tips they might have, and here they are:

10 safety tips for your next date

By Trish McDermott, VP Romance, Match.com

Match.com offers a fun and secure environment to meet other quality singles. It's also a great place to build loving and trusting friendships that can lead to lasting, offline relationships. Whether you decide to correspond online or meet members offline, please use sound judgment and be responsible for your conduct. In both the virtual and real worlds, common sense is your best safety tool.

1. **Start slow.** Watch out for someone who seems too good to be true. Begin by communicating solely via Match.com Messenger or email, then look for odd behavior or inconsistencies. The person at the other end may not be who or what he or she says. Trust your instincts. If anything makes you uncomfortable, walk away for your own safety and protection.

2. **Guard your anonymity.** All correspondence between Match.com members takes place through our double-blind system, ensuring your true identity is protected until you decide to reveal it. Never include your last name, email

address, home address, phone number, place of work or any other identifying information in your free profile or initial messages. When corresponding with another Match.com member, turn off your email signature file. Stop communicating with anyone who pressures you for personal information or attempts in any way to trick you into revealing it.

3. **Exercise caution and common sense.** Careful, thoughtful decisions generally yield better dating results. Guard against trusting the untrustworthy; suitors must earn your trust gradually, through consistently honorable, forthright behavior. Take all the time you need to test for a trustworthy person and pay careful attention along the way. If you suspect someone is lying, he or she probably is, so act accordingly. Be responsible about romance, and don't fall in love at the click of a mouse. Don't become prematurely intimate with someone, even if that intimacy only occurs online. If you mutually decide to cross the point of no return, be smart and protect yourself. The U.S. Centers for Disease Control and Prevention provide some of the most current information available about sexually transmitted diseases and preserving your health.

4. **Request a photo.** A photo will give you a good idea of the person's appearance, which may prove helpful in achieving a gut feeling. In fact, it's best to view several images of someone in various settings: casual, formal, indoor and outdoors. If all you hear are excuses about why you can't see a photo, consider that he or she has something to hide. Since Match.com offers free scanning services to its members, there's no reason someone shouldn't be able to provide you a photo.

5. **Chat on the phone.** A phone call can reveal much about a person's communication and social skills. Consider your security and do not reveal your personal phone number to a stranger. Try a cell phone number instead or use local telephone blocking techniques to prevent your phone number from appearing in Caller ID. Only furnish your phone number when you feel completely comfortable.

6. **Meet when YOU are ready.** The beauty of meeting and relating online is that you can collect information gradually, later choosing whether to pursue the relationship in the offline world. You never are obligated to meet anyone, regardless of your level of online intimacy. And even if you decide to arrange a meeting, you always have the right to change your mind. It's possible that your decision to keep the relationship at the anonymous level is based on a hunch that you can't logically explain. Trust yourself. Go with your instincts.

7. **Watch for red flags.** Pay attention to displays of anger, intense frustration or attempts to pressure or control you. Acting in a passive-aggressive manner, making demeaning or disrespectful comments, or any physically inappropriate behavior are all red flags. You should be concerned if your date exhibits any of the following behavior without providing an acceptable explanation:

   - Provides inconsistent information about age, interests, appearance, marital status, profession, employment, etc.
   - Refuses to speak to you on the phone after establishing ongoing, online intimacy.
   - Fails to provide direct answers to direct questions.

- Appears significantly different in person from his or her online persona.
- Never introduces you to friends, professional associates or family members.

8. **Meet in a safe place.** When you choose to meet offline, always tell a friend where you are going and when you will return. Leave your date's name and telephone number with your friend. Never arrange for your date to pick you up at home. Provide your own transportation, meet in a public place at a time with many people around, and when the date is over, leave on your own as well. A familiar restaurant or coffee shop, at a time when a lot of other people will be present, is often a fine choice. If you decide to move to another location, take your own car. When the timing is appropriate, thank your date for getting together and say goodbye.

9. **Take extra caution outside your area.** If you are flying in from another city, arrange for your own car and hotel room. Do not disclose the name of your hotel, and never allow your date to make the arrangements for you. Rent a car at the airport and drive directly to your hotel. Call your date from the hotel or meet at the location you have already agreed to. If the location seems inappropriate or unsafe, go back to your hotel. Try to contact your date at that location or leave a message on a home machine. Always make sure a friend or family member knows your plans and has your contact information. And if possible, carry a cell phone at all times.

10. **Get yourself out of a jam.** Never do anything you feel unsure about. If you are in any way afraid of your date, use your best judgment to diffuse the situation and get

out of there. Excuse yourself long enough to call a friend for advice, ask someone else on the scene for help, or slip out the back door and drive away. If you feel you are in danger, call the police; it's always better to be safe than sorry. Never worry or feel embarrassed about your behavior; your safety is much more important than one person's opinion of you.

While liars, cheaters, and imposters certainly ply their craft on the Web, you'll also find them in nightclubs and offline dating services, cocktail parties, or even sitting across from you at your local café. Regardless of where you meet someone, dating is never a risk-free activity, but a little caution will reduce your risk in matters of the heart.

I agree, dating is not risk free, but there are risks and there are risks. There's always the risk of winding up with a broken heart, but there shouldn't be any risks of bodily harm. So whatever you do, be as careful as possible.

Is dishonesty the best policy?

It's very tempting to be dishonest when dating on the Internet. It's easy to add an inch or two to your height or take off a pound or ten from your weight. Even if you post a picture, who says it shouldn't be one that's been touched up slightly to smooth out a wrinkle or two.

Now even people who meet do some camouflaging. Women wear makeup and supporting undergarments while men may comb their hair in a certain way or suck in their gut as much as possible. It's okay to give in to the natural instinct to put your best foot forward. But while it's okay to take one small step, don't go further than that.

If the two of you hit it off online and you decide to meet, you don't want the other party to be disappointed. Remember, first impressions count, and if you've built yourself up to a point where the first impression you're going to make in person is negative, as compared to your online persona, you'll have lost before you even had a chance to begin.

I'm not saying you have to be totally honest. You can smooth off some edges, because the other person will probably be doing the same and so will discount some of what you say anyway. Just don't go over the top so you later regret what you've done.

When to do "it"

A big question everybody has is when to have sex in the dating process. Many people want to put a number on it; after so many dates it's time to have sex. I say that's nonsense. Each couple is made up of two unique individuals and the circumstances will also be unique. Given this situation, you can't expect to say that you must be having sex by the fourth or sixth or twentieth date. There's enough pressure in dating without adding even more with artificial deadlines.

The decision of when to have sex is therefore something unique that each couple has to decide for themselves. There's certainly going to be some feeling out each other's position, as there always is when people date.

There's nothing wrong with laying out some ground rules ahead of time, if you want to so there's no confusion. But don't let such an artificial deadline hold you back if things are progressing faster and better than you thought was going to happen. While it's true you don't want to regret having done something, you also don't want to regret not having done it either.

Too old for sex?

I've covered this in an earlier chapter, but I want to talk about it a little bit again, because it is so important and because it often comes up when people have begun dating again after a long period of being part of a couple.

Because our society puts so much emphasis on the young, the truth that older people have sex and enjoy it tends to get overlooked. In fact, for some reason, there's an undercurrent of belief that older people having sex is icky, maybe even something that shouldn't be done.

This societal attitude can affect older people's attitudes toward older people having sex—including themselves. If you buy into the assumption you should be sexless, then that's going to diminish your sexuality. It's ironic. Young people are pushed towards having sex before they want to, in part because of peer pressure, and older people end up being pushed away from having sex, because of society's attitude.

Neither situation is right, and you shouldn't let yourself be pressured into not having sex any more than a teen should allow himself or herself to be pressured into having it. We're all sexual beings and we should admit it. If you're with a partner and you feel aroused, don't stifle those urges. Encourage them, in yourself and in each other. Sex can bring great benefits, and you deserve them no matter what your age.

STDs

Having given you these encouraging words, I now have to put in a caveat. While older adults may not have to face the risks of an unintended pregnancy (as long as the older adult isn't a male having sex with a younger female adult), the risks of transmitting a sexually transmitted disease remain.

I've read that there's an interesting pattern that sometimes develops with older adults who live in communities. In some of these communities there's a lot of dating that goes on, and hence there's a fair amount of sex that takes place between the members of the community. If all the members are STD-free, there's little risk of catching an STD. However, if even one member of the community has an STD, in a short amount of time, that STD can spread very quickly. Of course, even in one of these "safe" communities, if one member has sex outside of the community, an STD could easily be introduced.

Safer-sex difficulties

Let me state that there's no such thing as safe sex between singles. There is always some element of risk, which is why I only use the term "safer sex." But certainly people can engage in safer sex and reduce the risks. As you probably know, the number one form of protection is condoms, although they don't offer 100 percent protection. They can break, fall off, or, in the case of some diseases like herpes, don't cover all the potentially affected areas. But they're far better than nothing and should be used whenever you're having sex with someone that you are not sure has a 100 percent clean bill of health. This is a message that has gotten through to the younger generations and condom usage is way up among them. But it meets with a lot more resistance among older adults.

There are several reasons for this. The first is that the condom is also a method of preventing unintended pregnancies. Since pregnancy is not a risk for most older adults, some people just think it's silly to have to use them. That's especially true if they believe, however wrongly, that STDs aren't particularly prevalent among older adults.

STDs aren't affected by people's ages. Transmission is related to how many partners you and your partners have. So while an older married adult may not have any STDs, especially if both parties remained virgins until they were married and faithful since, older adults that have sex with multiple partners are very much at risk.

And there's a factor here that's at play with older adults and condoms. Older men have more difficulties obtaining and maintaining erections. Those with severe problems can, if their doctors permit it, take a pill. But there are men who don't need a pill but who actually do have problems or think they have problems with their erections if they are forced to wear a condom.

It's true older men need more stimulation and condoms lessen the sensations, but, while I don't have any scientific information to back me up, in my opinion, many of the men who say this are using it as an excuse. They don't like condoms, they feel silly using a condom at their age, so they say they can't use a condom.

Here's where demographics come into play. If there were just as many single women as single men, the women could easily refuse to have sex with any male who refused to wear a condom and still be able to find a sex partner. But, because the older a woman gets, the less her chances of finding a partner, that puts her in a dicey position.

If she refuses to have sex with a man because he won't wear a condom, he won't have much of a problem of finding himself another partner, but she might. And since every older woman knows this, they're all forced to give serious consideration to this pressure not to use condoms. What is an older woman to do? Simply give up and have sex without a condom, accepting the risk that she'll get some STD, or dig her heels in and insist on a condom, possibly losing any chance of ever having sex again?

Let me offer two other possible solutions, neither of which is 100 percent satisfactory, but perhaps still worth considering.

The first one is based on the fact that not every one of these men who refuse to wear a condom is mean-spirited, but rather they sincerely fear having erectile problems while wearing a condom. You might not be able to get him to change his mind, but you might have an easier time getting him to be checked for STDs.

In other words, I don't think these men want to spread disease. So to make up for the added risk they're putting you through, there's a good chance they'll have themselves checked out. Now just because a man can produce a doctor's certification that he has a clean bill of health does not eliminate the risk because, if he doesn't remain faithful to you, he could catch something subsequent to being tested that he could then pass on to you. Yet, if you know the gentlemen fairly well, perhaps that's an acceptable risk.

The other road you could follow is not to have actual intercourse. Is there a risk you could catch an STD through oral sex? Yes, but it is lower than through vaginal sex. So, again, you'd be lowering the odds, not as low as you could with a condom, but not as high as having vaginal sex without a condom. And since older men sometimes do have problems with their erections, oral sex might actually be better for them, since a woman can give a man more stimulation with her mouth and tongue than she can with her vagina.

Another advantage of going this route is that by giving him oral sex, you're in a better position to get oral sex back, which is more likely to lead to your having an orgasm than is vaginal sex. And there's also manual sex, which would reduce the risk of transmission to almost zero, though not everyone may find this solution satisfactory.

As I said, these added options aren't perfect, but they are options. They give women some bargaining room so that it's not an either-or situation. Of course, if you are a woman and any risk of picking up an STD is too high for you, there are always vibrators. Turn to the next chapter for more information on the subject of solo sex.

12
Solo Sex

Anyone, of any age, can find himself or herself without a partner, but as I've already pointed out, the odds of turning this situation around worsen as you get older, particularly if you're a woman, as there are many more older women than older men. But even people with partners, including married people, masturbate. So although this chapter may be called "Solo Sex," it's not just for singles. It is for anyone who finds the need for sexual stimulation and no available or willing partner.

Masturbation, perhaps more than any other sexual act, is one that is linked with guilt. You might think, since masturbation is the only form of truly safe sex and since it causes harm to no one, that the guilt factor would be minimal. And yet just the opposite is true.

Some of this guilt stems from Biblical times, though in fact there is some misunderstanding about that. The word for masturbation in many languages has as a root the word "onan." In the Bible, Onan sinned by spilling his seed on the ground. Only Onan didn't masturbate. His brother died and, according to the Jewish laws of his time, he was supposed to impregnate his sister-in-law. Instead he used coitus interruptus; he pulled his penis out of her vagina before ejaculating. But he did spill his seed, and the same occurs whenever a man masturbates. (According to this logic, women could masturbate all they want since they have no seed to spill. But society's attitude towards masturbation often makes many women feel even more guilty than men.)

Whether or not people have drawn the wrong conclusion based on the story of Onan isn't really relevant because the result has been that masturbation has long been looked at as a sin. That hasn't stopped people from indulging in this form of sexual pleasure. What it has done, with many people, is add a touch of guilt to every such act. I'm here to tell you to forget about this guilt, although with a couple of caveats.

The first has to do with religion. I'm a believer, and I don't want it said I ever encouraged anyone to break the laws of their religion. Those people who truly believe this act is wrong should listen to their conscience and refrain from masturbating. After all, nobody ever died because of sexual frustration. (It just sometimes feels like you're going to.)

Many religious bans stem from a real danger that became absorbed into a religious tenet. The ban on eating pork followed by Jews and Muslims, for example, originated because, in ancient times, eating pork carried the danger of disease. Masturbation also carries with it some dangers, though of a different variety.

In Biblical times, it was important to have a large family, because your children formed the safety net for your old age, a primitive retirement plan if you will. And since not every child was going to live to adulthood, couples had to make sure to have plenty of offspring to insure there were some left to take care of them. Now someone who was using up all of his or her sexual energy masturbating was less likely to be procreating, and this created the potential for sociological trouble in the form of old people without any family to care for them. So, not only was marriage encouraged, but masturbation was discouraged.

If you're over fifty, issues of childbearing aren't really relevant anyway, especially if you are a woman. And today we have other methods of ensuring our well-being in our later years such as the U.S. Social Security system (embattled though it is), individual retirement accounts, and company pensions. With these issues put aside, you should be able to masturbate all you want without any guilt. However there is another peril that remains.

If you don't have a partner, any sexual frustration you might feel should be used as an incentive to find someone to share your life with. Older woman could say to themselves, "There's no point looking for a partner because there aren't enough to go around" and merely masturbate. But a woman who chose not to masturbate and to channel her sexual frustration into seeking out companionship a little more aggressively than the other women out there would be more likely to succeed. So to some degree it's one of those Catch-22 situations.

My recommendation is to meet this dilemma half way. If you are single and feel sexually frustrated, you should, if your religious beliefs allow, masturbate. But you shouldn't do it to such an extent you lose all your incentive to find a partner. Or, if you do masturbate a lot, make a pledge to yourself not to give up on the chase. It may seem impossible, but it's not—unless you give up. (See the preceding chapter on finding a partner for help in this regard.)

Permission to masturbate

This whole issue of giving yourself permission to masturbate may not seem like such a big deal to anyone who has already masturbated, but I am often asked by older adults, particularly women, about just this issue. If you have always had a sexual partner and have never masturbated and you now find yourself alone, you may be facing masturbation as a serious option for the first time. But, if when you try to masturbate you begin experiencing feelings of guilt or shame, failure to achieve satisfaction becomes a real possibility.

As I've said many times in this book, the main sexual organ is the brain, not the genitals. You need both, but if the brain is sabotaging matters, you can stimulate the genitals all you want and it's not going to work. Guilt and shame are two powerful emotions that can act as saboteurs.

If you feel something like this is occurring, but you want to masturbate, you have to trick your brain into cooperating. By trick I mean you have to overwhelm it with sexual thoughts that will block out the negative emotions. That's one reason people use erotica when masturbating.

Visual images work quite effectively with men, and the marketplace has provided for this need with a flood of material that contains erotic images. Some women also find such images stimulating, but not all. Older women may have a particular problem with erotica because it usually features young buxom women, which could prove more threatening than arousing to a woman with an aging body. On the other hand, there is erotic material they might find quite arousing including books (as I've mentioned, one of my favorites is *Lady Chatterley's Lover*), collections of short stories, and films that have been produced by women.

Using fantasy

Another way of achieving the same end without resorting to outside influences is the use of fantasy. Fantasies are usually quite personal, which is why they may work better for some people. You could spend some time—an hour or an afternoon—working on a fantasy, honing all the details. Then, whenever you were ready to masturbate, which might be right after all this sexual creativity but could be later, you'd be able to lose yourself in this fantasy so any attempts by your brain to sabotage matters would be pushed aside.

My Secret Garden

For those of you who find yourself fantasy-challenged, that is to say not sure of exactly what an erotic fantasy consists of, I would recommend a book by Nancy Friday entitled *My Secret Garden*. Nancy assembled the fantasies of many people in this book and not only might you find it educational, but quite arousing in and of itself. If after reading this book or one of Nancy's other compilations of fantasies (*Forbidden Flowers, Women On Top* or *Men In Love*) you find you don't need to create your own fantasy because this material was sufficient to allow you to masturbate, great. But if other people's fantasies don't make you excited, or the very act of reading ends up being a distraction, then, as I've suggested, use these fantasies as a template to create your own.

Masturbating techniques—male

In general, men don't have many problems masturbating. They're used to handling their penis, because they have to do it every time they urinate. And the part of their penis that is the most sensitive, which in general is the front underside around the frenulum, though that can vary, is easily touched. The majority of men simply use their hand to rub up and down the shaft of their penis. Some men use a lubricant, like Vaseline or a hand cream, to avoid irritating the penis. Using a lubricant also allows a man to use his whole hand, making the experience more like intercourse. Others prefer not to use a lubricant and use only their fingers for a gentler touch.

Men can masturbate standing up, sitting down, or lying down. Each man usually develops his own technique. Those men who use a lubricant may rub very vigorously, while those who prefer the "dry" technique will tend to be more gentle.

Some men will also stroke their testicles, perineum (the "seam" which runs between the legs), or anus at the same time they are rubbing their penis. In general, men will develop one technique and stick to it rather than trying different types of routines, though that's not true of every man.

Some men prefer to rub their penis up against an object, like a pillow. They'll lie on their stomachs and rub up and down against this object, simulating the movements of intercourse.

There are devices for men, artificial vaginas if you will, that can be used for masturbation. Some of these are attached to inflat-

Tip:

It may be tempting to use someone you know as the central figure of a sexual fantasy. I understand this could make the fantasy seem more believable because it could potentially happen and therefore is more arousing, but there's a downside to this. You could get so involved with this fantasy you end up trying to make it real. If you're fantasizing about a coworker or next-door neighbor, for example, even if this person is married and unavailable to you, you could find yourself flirting with him or her. You could find yourself mixing your fantasies with your real life, and that's not a good idea. You'll end up with emotional ties to this person, making it difficult for you to go out and look for a potential real partner.

To avoid this risk, I would suggest you use someone completely unavailable to you as the central figure in your fantasy, like a movie or TV star. That way you'll be able to keep your two feet on the ground and keep your fantasy life and your real life completely separate.

able dolls, helping the man to fantasize he is actually having inter-course with a woman.

Some men use a vibrator to stimulate their penis, though most will find a vibrator on a bare penis offers so much stimulation as to be painful. But by wrapping the vibrator in a towel or adding a sleeve made especially for the penis that attaches to some vibrators, the sensations can be toned down to a pleasurable level. The jets of a Jacuzzi or from a hand-held shower head can also cause the right sensations to cause an orgasm.

Speed

Masturbation is not supposed to be a race to the finish, but many men do rush through it. Speculation is this habit stems from young boys wanting to get it over with to minimize the risk of getting caught. As a kind of aside, it's possible that, having gotten used to rushing, many of these boys, when they grow up and have sex with women, end up having problems with premature ejaculation. While there's no proof for this, it does make sense, and so my advice to any man who is masturbating and doesn't have to rush is to slow the pace down as much as possible. Of course premature ejaculation is less of a problem with older men.

Women can face the opposite problem. If masturbation starts to take too long, a woman's thoughts may begin to stray. If she finds herself distracted, thinking about other matters, she won't be able to have an orgasm at all. It's at moments like these that a woman has to be able to dive deep into her sexual fantasy so she can refocus her thoughts on arousing stimuli. It's also the reason women need to have more time put aside for masturbation.

A man with five minutes to spare can potentially use it to mas-turbate successfully. But if a woman feels pressured by time con-

225

straints, she probably won't be successful. That's why most women need to be able to set aside a block of time without the risk of being interrupted, if they're going to be successful at reaching an orgasm through masturbation.

Techniques for women

Like men, a woman can simply use her hand to stimulate her genital area. I say genital area rather than clitoris, because some women find an aroused clitoris too sensitive for actual touching. There are women who feel this way right from the beginning, while others find their clitoris becomes more sensitive the more aroused they are. In such cases, the woman needs to stimulate the area around her clitoris, which will give some stimulation to the clitoris itself, but not so much as to be uncomfortable.

It may take a woman a while to discover exactly what type of stroking will cause her to have an orgasm, as this is a very personal variable.

(This is why I say to women who have difficulties having an orgasm with a man that they must first learn how to give themselves an orgasm so they can then teach their partner what to do. There is no way for the man to guess whether or not he is giving the correct stimulation, especially as it can change according to the level of the woman's arousal.)

Just remember, there is no wrong way to masturbate. As long as some series of strokes provides the desired result, it makes no difference what she actually does.

When more is needed

Some women cannot provide themselves with enough stimulation using just their hands and fingers. They'll be touching themselves for such a long time that they can't keep themselves from getting distracted, or else they seem to approach having an orgasm but never quite get there. Those women require the extra stimulation of a vibrator. For some women this added stimulation is needed only when they masturbate, for others it is required any time they want an orgasm, with or without a partner.

There are many different kinds of vibrators. There are small battery operated ones and larger ones which plug into the wall and provide stronger sensations. I've endorsed one brand, the Eroscillator, that oscillates instead of vibrates, which tests have shown to be even more effective. There are vibrators that strap on, so a woman could use it under her clothes without anyone knowing, as long as they weren't within earshot.

Since there are so many different types, I would suggest anyone considering purchasing one consult either a Web site or a catalogue. If you live in the United States, two companies I can recommend are Eve's Garden and Good Vibrations, though there are many others. (See the "Resources" section at the back of the book for contact information.) From these companies you'll learn which vibrators are the most reliable, but only personal experience will tell you which one works best for you.

📌 Tip:

There are some body massagers which can also act as a vibrator. You might want to purchase one of these to see whether or not you like this type of sensation. If it turns out you really don't, at least you can use the machine for its intended purpose of massaging sore muscles.

Dildos

While the center of a woman's orgasm is her clitoris, that doesn't mean women don't enjoy the feeling of having something inside them when they are masturbating. A dildo is a hard, penis-shaped device that a woman can insert into her vagina during masturbation. Not all dildos resemble a penis exactly. They come in a variety of imaginative designs including the dolphin-shaped one I mentioned earlier that is often preferred by lesbians.

Many women have found you don't need to purchase devices made to be dildos, as there are fruits, vegetables, candles, and other objects which can be used for the same purpose.

No matter what you use, just be certain to wash it carefully before inserting it into your vagina. Soap and water work well, or you could clean it with rubbing alcohol and then carefully rinse the alcohol off.

If you begin to insert the object before you are fully aroused and lubricated, or, if you are a woman who doesn't make very much natural lubrication, coat the object with one of the lubricants before attempting to insert it.

Water works

Because men must handle their penis regularly, they rarely have any hesitation when it comes to masturbation. In fact, as we discussed, there are those men to whom masturbation becomes too tempting, and they spend far too much time pleasuring themselves.

But women aren't as familiar with their genitals as men are. And if, when they were young, they took to heart the parental admonition not to touch themselves "down there," they may have psychological difficulties with hands-on masturbation later in life.

Remember, a woman's ability to become aroused can be fragile, which is why any such learned beliefs could pose a serious stumbling block.

Some women discovered that a way of getting around this block is to masturbate without directly touching themselves. One such method involves keeping your underpants on and rubbing through the material. Another substitutes a stream of water to stimulate the clitoris instead of your fingers.

In the days before hand-held shower heads were common, the technique many used was to lie down in the tub, scoot themselves under the faucet, with their legs up against the bath wall, so the flow of water from the faucet fell right where it gave the most pleasure. With the invention of hand-held shower heads, many with all sorts of pulsating sprays, the need for such acrobatics declined, though some women still prefer the old-fashioned method if they've become used to it over the years. Those who have hot tubs may find the jets can also act as an intense source of pleasure.

My view

From my point of view, whatever works is absolutely fine. The use of water does have one particular drawback, which is that it must be performed in the bathroom or in a hot tub. If using water as a means to stimulate the clitoris is the only way a woman can have an orgasm, this issue must be integrated into the relationship. The woman and her partner can make love in any other room of the house during foreplay and to satisfy his needs, but at some point they must visit the one place where she can be sexually satisfied.

There was a time when many women never achieved sexual satisfaction. Sex was looked upon as a duty to be fulfilled, both to satisfy the husband and to make babies. A percentage of women accepted that role, however willingly, and went through life never once getting that feeling of being sexually satisfied. Many were sexually frustrated but didn't know what to do about it. They didn't get sexual satisfaction from having sex with their partner, and they couldn't bring themselves to masturbate.

Today we know just about any woman can achieve sexual satisfaction. In most cases her partner can be taught what to do. But some women can only have an orgasm with precise stimulation, perhaps only when self-administered. Is this a handicap? Yes, let's be truthful. But how many of us don't have perfect vision and require artificial lenses? Or hearing aids, canes, or a wide assortment of pills? In other words, many of us are handicapped to some degree, especially as we advance in age.

Isn't it better to try to get the most satisfaction out of life rather than live a life of frustration? If anyone requires special means to achieve sexual satisfaction, that person deserves the respect we give everyone else, particularly from a partner. So if you don't already know, find out what you require to have sexual satisfaction; and whether alone or with a partner, make sure you fulfill this very human need.

Resources

There is lots of information on the Internet, though when it comes to sex, much of it may lead to material that you might not want to view. I've tried to do my best to keep you away from sites that might be offensive, but since there's a good chance that some of this information may have changed by the time it gets into your hands, I can't guarantee it. And after all, this is a book about sex so you shouldn't run into anything too shocking, at least as long as you don't click on anything that may appear to lead to a triple-X-rated site.

On the other hand, if you're curious about some of these sites that feature erotica and don't know where to start, let me recommend www.janesguide.com. In this site are reviews of sites that feature sexual material. By reading the descriptions, you may narrow your focus before actually clicking on anything. You'll also be told which sites offer free material and which ask for payment. Please be aware that some of the sites that ask for payment are not run by scrupulous people. So there is a risk in giving your credit card number, or any information or even calling an 800 number, on these sites. And just because a reviewer from Janesguide got away without any problems doesn't guarantee that you will too.

Since I realize that not everyone is connected to cyberspace, where possible and appropriate I've also given you addresses and phone numbers. And if you continue further down, you'll find a list of books.

Counseling
- American Association for Marriage and Family Therapy, 112 South Alfred Street, Alexandria, VA 22314, 703-838-9808, www.aamft.org
- American Mental Health Counselor's Association, 801 N.

Fairfax Street, Suite 304, Alexandria, VA 22314, 800-326-2642, www.amhca.org

• American Psychiatric Association,1000 Wilson Blvd., Suite 1825, Arlington, VA 22209; 703-907-7300; www.psych.org

• American Psychological Association, 750 First St. NE, Washington, DC 20002; 202-336-5500; www.apa.org

• Associations of Gay and Lesbian Psychiatrists, 4514 Chester Avenue, Philadelphia, PA 19143; 215-222-2800; www.aglp.org

• American Association of Pastoral Counselors, 9504A Lee Highway, Fairfax, VA 22031; 703-385-6967; www.aapc.org

Sex Therapy and Sex Study

AASECT (American Association of Sex Educators, Counselors and Therapists), P.O. Box 5488, Richmond, VA 23220; 804-644-3288; www.aasect.org

• American Board of Sexology, 2431 Aloma Avenue, Suite 277, Winter Park, FL 32792; 407-645-1641; www.sexologist.org

• Kinsey Institute; www.indiana.edu/%7ekinsey/

• Society For Human Sexuality; www.sexuality.org

• Society for the Study of Sexuality, P.O. Box 416, Allentown, PA 18105; 610-530-2483; www.sexscience.org

Health

• Centers for Disease Control and Prevention's National STD/AIDS Hotline, 800-342-AIDS or 800-227-8922; 1600 Clifton Road, Atlanta, GA 30333; 404-639-3311, 800-311-3435

• Sexual Function Health Council /American Foundation for Urologic Disease,1000 Corporate Boulevard, Suite 410, Linthicum, MD 21090; 410-689-3990; email: impotence@afud.org; Internet: www.impotence.org

• American Urological Association, 1000 Corporate Blvd., Linthicum, MD 21090; 866-RING-AUA (746-4282) or 410-689-3700; email: aua@auanet.org; Internet: www.auanet.org

AUA can refer you to a urologist in your area.

• American Diabetes Association (ADA) National Office,1701 North Beauregard Street, Alexandria, VA 22311; 800-DIABETES (342-2383); www.diabetes.org

ADA can help you find a doctor who specializes in diabetes care in your area.

• Impotence Anonymous and I-ANON Chapters, 800-669-1603. Callers can receive list of urologists who have the latest treatment options for impotency as well as local support groups.

• Impotence World Association (IWA), 10400 Little Patuxent Parkway, Suite 485, Columbia, MD, 21044-3502. Send three dollars to above address with request for educational materials or referral lists of local physicians and therapists who treat impotency.

• www.impotence.org. Sponsored by the American Foundation For Urological Disease Inc. Site has lots of useful information and a good set of links to other sites for additional information.

• www.hisandherhealth.com. This site was put together by a urologist and contains some interesting and useful information.

• www.impotencespecialists.com. This is a good site if you're looking for a specialist and to get information.

• HIV Over Fifty; www.hivoverfifty.org

Sexual Toys

Adam & Eve, P.O. Box 8200, Hillsborough, NC 27278; 919-644-8100; www.adameve.com

• Condomania; 800-9-CONDOM; www.condomania.com

• Eve's Garden, 119 West 57th St., Suite 1201, New York, NY 10019; 800-848-3837; www.evesgarden.com

• Good Vibrations, 938 Howard St., San Francisco, CA 94103; 800-289-8423; www.goodvibes.com

• Sinclair Intimacy Institute, P.O. Box 8865, Chapel Hill, NC 27515; 800-955-0888; www.bettersex.com. In addition to being able to purchase sex toys and erotica, there is a very good sex dictionary on this site.

• www.eroscillator.com. Vibrators vibrate. The Eroscillator oscillates, and many women find the sensations stronger and more arousing. I was approached by the manufacturer, and I had a sociologist friend do some research. The women who were part of the test reported that they found it better than other such devices and so I agreed to endorse it. If you want to learn more, visit their website.

Senior Sites

www.findingloveafter50.com
www.seniorjournal.com
www.seniorsite.com
www.suddenlysenior.com
www.seniorcupid.com
www.seniorliving.miningco.com

Miscellaneous

• www.goaskalice.columbia.edu. Though started for students, this site has been around for many years giving factual information, and there's much to learn for someone of any age combing through the various topics that have been covered.

• And if you go to www.drruth.com, you'll be connected to my message boards on iVillage.com. In addition to whatever posts are there currently, you can find past posts that cover many subjects, though I don't answer all the questions. There is also a lot of good information on iVillage if you poke around, and not only about sex and relationships.

Books

The Merck Manual. This textbook is a good source for basic information on just about every aspect of medicine. It is available online at:

http://www.merck.com/mrkshared/mmanual/section3/sec3.jsp

• ***For Yourself: The Fulfillment of Female Sexuality*** by Lonnie Barbach, Ph.D. Signet Book. This is a book I've recommended for years to women who have problems having orgasms.

• ***The Joy of Sex: Fully Revised & Completely Updated for the 21st Century*** by Alex Comfort. Crown. This is a revised edition of the classic book first published in 1979. I still recommend it to clients who want to learn about new sexual positions. You'll find a lot more positions in the Kama Sutra, of which there are many editions, but let's face it, many of those are impossible unless you've got hidden acrobatic skills.

• ***Sex For Dummies*** by Dr. Ruth Westheimer. I cover every base in this book, and the format is fun and easy to flip around.

• ***Good Vibrations Guide to Sex: The Most Complete Sex Manual Ever Written*** by Cathy Winks and Anne Semens. Cleis Press. A large book with a lot of information.

• ***Guide to Getting It On!: The Universe's Coolest and Most Informative Book About Sex for Adults of All Ages*** by Paul Joannides and Daerick Gross, Sr. Goofy Foot Press. This book is playfully written but you can find some practical information about certain positions that is not easily found elsewhere. Be aware that the illustrations are quite graphic. This is not a book to be left where children might find it.

• ***My Secret Garden*** by Nancy Friday. Pocket Books.

• ***Forbidden Flowers*** by Nancy Friday. Pocket Books.

• ***Women On Top*** by Nancy Friday. Pocket Books.

• As I stated in the book, Nancy Friday has written compilations of fantasies that are quite arousing.

• ***The New Male Sexuality, Revised Edition***by Bernie Zilbergeld. Bantam.

• ***The New Love and Sex After 60*** by Robert N. Butler and Myrna I. Lewis. Ballantine Books.

• ***A Celebration of Sex After 50*** by Douglas E. Rosenau, James K. Childerston and Carolyn Childerston. Nelson Books.

• ***Dating After 50*** by Sharon Romm, M.D. Quill Driver Books. A great guide for getting back into the dating scene if you find yourself single again.

Index

Acknowledgments

To the memory of my entire family who perished during the Holocaust. To the memory of my late husband, Fred, who encouraged me in all my endeavors. To my current family, my daughter Miriam Westheimer, Ed.D., son-in-law Joel Einleger, M.B.A., their children Ari and Leora, my son Joel Westheimer, Ph.D., daughter-in-law Barabara Leckie, Ph.D., and their children Michal and Benjamin. I have the best grandchildren in the entire world!

Thanks to all the many family members and friends for adding so much to my life. I'd need an entire chapter to list them all but some must be mentioned here: Pierre Lehu and I have now collaborated on a dozen books, he's the best Minister of Communications I could have asked for! Cliff Rubin, my assistant, thanks! Ruth Bachrach, Commisioner Adrian Benepe, Peter Berger, M.D., David Best, M.D., Chuck Blazer, Carlita C. de Chavez, Marcie Citron, Glynn Cohen, Hersh Cohen, Martin Englisher, Cynthia Fuchs Epstein, Ph.D., Howard Epstein, Josh Gaspero, David Goslin, Ph.D., Elliot Horowitz, Fred Howard, Vera Jelinek, Alfred Kaplan, Steve Kaplan, Ph.D., Michael Kassan, Amy Kassiola, Joel Kassiola, Ph.D., Bonnie Kaye, Richard and Barbara Kendall, Robert Krasner, M.D., Marga and Bill Kunreuther, Phil & Linda Lader, Dean Stephen Lassonde, Rabbi and Mrs. William Lebeau, Mark Lebwohl, M.D., Lou Lieberman, Ph.D. and Mary Cuadrado, Ph.D., John and Ginger Lollos, Amb. & Mrs. Raymond Loretan, Frank Luntz, Doug McCormick, Dale Ordes, Henry & Sydelle Ostberg, Bruce Paisner, Robert Pinto, Commissioner Ken Podziba, Philip Prioleau, M.D., Bob Rose, Fred and Anne Rosenberg, Larry Ruvo, Simeon and Rose Schreiber, Daniel Schwartz, Amir Shaviv, John and Marianne Slade, Betsy Sledge, William Sledge, M.D., Hannah Strauss, Jeff Tabak, Esq., Malcolm Thomson, Markus Wilhelm, Greg Willenborg, Ben Yagoda, Froma Zeitlin, Ph.D. and Ed ZollaAnd to all of the people who worked so hard to bring this book into print at Quill Driver Books especially Steve Mettee, Doris Hall, and Mary Ann Gardner.

About the Authors

Dr. Ruth Westheimer is a psychosexual therapist who pioneered the field of media therapy. She is currently an adjunct professor at N.Y.U. and a fellow of both Calhoun College at Yale and Butler College at Princeton as well as a fellow of the New York Academy of Medicine. She has her own private practice in New York and lectures worldwide.

She is the author of thirty books and has her own web page (www.drruth.com.) Dr. Westheimer has two children, four grandchildren and resides in New York City.

Pierre Lehu has been Dr. Westheimer's minister of communications for nearly twenty-five years. This is the thirteenth book on which he has collaborated with her. He lives in New York and is married with two children.

Other Great Books in

The Best Half of Life® Series

ISBN 1-884956-35-1

Live Longer, Live Better
Taking Care of Your Health After 50
by Peter H. Gott, M.D.

America's most widely read medical columnist
(350 newspapers nationwide)

$14.95 *($23.50Canada)*

Peter H. Gott, M.D. combines the empathy of an old-fashioned family doctor with the outspoken fervor of a patients' rights advocate and dispenses advice on a plethora of health concerns aimed at keeping his readers healthy and active.

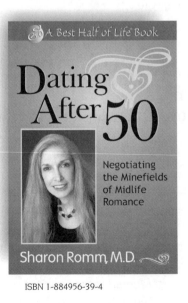

ISBN 1-884956-39-4

Dating After 50
Negotiating the Minefields of Mid-Life Romance
—by Sharon Romm, M.D.
$12.95 ($19.95 Canada)

Dating often seems scary, especially if you haven't dated in a long time, but it can be manageable and even fun if you remember to go at your own pace and stay in your comfort zone. Think of it as similar to a job search in which you are looking for a good fit between your interests and requirements and the needs of your potential companion.

In *Dating After 50*, readers will learn the safest and most efficient way to find dates, but the story doesn't end once they've planned a second date. Expect sound advice on managing second families, jealousy, former spouses, rejection, money, benefits, retirement and a host of other issues common to later-life relationships.

Other Great Books in

The Best Half of Life® Series

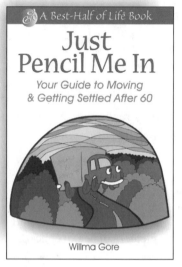

ISBN 1-884956-21-1

Just Pencil Me In

Your Guide to Moving & Getting Settled After 60

by Willma Willis Gore

$12.95 ($19.95 Canada)

While moving never is simple, moving after one has reached the age of 60 often presents its own special challenges. Yet, it also offers its own special rewards— it's a chance to simplify one's life, to kind of clear out the cellar, both literally and figuratively. It's an opportunity to meet new people, to visit new places, and to learn new things. In fact, with proper planning and execution, moving can and will be an enjoyable adventure.

Just Pencil Me In addresses the unique, distinct concerns encountered by those of us over 60 when faced with relocating. Smooths the way to making your move uncomplicated and enjoyable.

ISBN 1-884956-15-7

The Memory Manual

10 Simple Things You Can Do to Improve Your Memory After *50*

By Betty Fielding

$14.95 ($21.95 Canada)

- Tired of looking for where you left your car keys?
- Embarrassed when you forget the name of someone you've just met?
- Wish you could remember more details about what you read?

Then *The Memory Manual* is the book for you! No gimmicks, no long codes or systems to study and memorize, just a simple, holistic program that will get you or a loved one on track to a better memory and a fuller life!